~ A MEMOIR ~

Meeting *Life's* Challenges

BROOKS C WILSON

Ark House Press
arkhousepress.com

Cataloguing in Publication Data:
Title: Meeting Life's Challenges
ISBN: 978-0-6455535-8-1 (pbk)
Subjects: Memoirs; Christian Living; Business;
Other Authors/Contributors: Wilson, Brooks C.
Design by initiateagency.com

Reflections on my life, my family
and the times in which I lived

CONTENTS

Brooks Christian Wilson, AM

DEDICATION

To
my wife Ann
with whom
I shared my life for 61 years.

FOREWORD

I am considerably older than Brooks Wilson and after a long and happy marriage like him I now live alone, and Brooks has asked me to write the Foreword to this book.

The story begins when he was about four years old and contains many of his and his wife Ann's memories of growing up, meeting in America, falling in love, marrying, and travelling the world together looking for employment, discovery and adventure.

The account of those times also took me on a voyage of discovery, resulting in my realization that the elderly friend I now have in Brooks Wilson is one of the most remarkable men I have known in my long life.

Marsden Hordern
Warrawee
April 2022

PREFACE

This is the story of my life. I have written it so that future generations will know about the times in which I lived and the challenges I faced.

It is my hope that aspects of my story might help those who come after me.

I am now eighty-nine. As I look at life, I realize it is a fleeting experience. None of us asked to be born, yet we were. We all inherit the genes of our parents. We grow up, go to school, and may receive further education if we are fortunate. We get a job, get married, have a family, and ultimately, we die. One generation leads to the next. The difference in the life experience between the generations is caused by the times in which we live.

In whatever period we are born, we all live in the same beautiful place called Planet Earth. We have air to breath and food to eat. Our common challenge is to lead a useful life so that when our time is up, we leave the world a better place.

How do we do this?

In my opinion, there are two ways.

The first is to get the best education we can so that we subsequently have a job that enables us to earn a living and help others at the same time.

The second, and more important, is to be a good parent so the next generation grows up knowing they are totally loved.

Receiving this total love gives a deep sense of security that lasts a lifetime.

Paul spoke about love in his letter to the Corinthians:

"Love is patient, love is kind. It does not envy, it does not boast, it is not proud. It does not dishonor others. It is not self-seeking, it is not easily angered, it keeps no records of wrongs".

Life is not all about "us". The key is to forget "self" and reach out to others.

To illustrate this point, in chapter 11 I tell the life story of two of my great-grandfathers who were born around 1830. One was born in Ireland and the other in the United States. They each faced major difficulties in their early lives that they overcame with the help and love of family. They then went ahead and led useful lives, leaving behind families of their own.

We can learn from their experiences.

To all my relatives and friends who might read this book, thank you for being part of my life.

Brooks C. Wilson
Warrawee
April 2022

ACKNOWLEDGEMENTS

There are many people who helped me write this book.

The first person to mention is my wife Ann who had written a story about her own life. I was able to draw on what she had written.

Then our children, Charles, John, Mary and Andrew, each added information about our family life and their role in it.

My sister Sally encouraged me to write this book, and my sister Robin sent me family photos from her collection.

Reaching further afield my cousin, Snow Thomas, in Tasmania, provided information about his family property North Down which is where my Great Grandfather, Henry John Wilson, lived and married after he arrived in Australia in 1852.

Information about my American Great Grandfather, William Eustis Brooks, was sent to me by my cousin, John Brooks, who lives in Maine. He had in his collection a book outlining the life of William Eustice Brooks published after his death in 1906.

In putting all this together my son, Andrew Wilson, played a key role. He helped format what I had written and he was able to select and digitize the photos I have used.

Finally, I would like to acknowledge the work of Lorraine Purcell in editing what I had written. She played a similar role in a book I wrote about my father.

Teri Kempe also played a key role in getting this book published.

My thanks to everyone.

CHAPTER 1

My Early Years

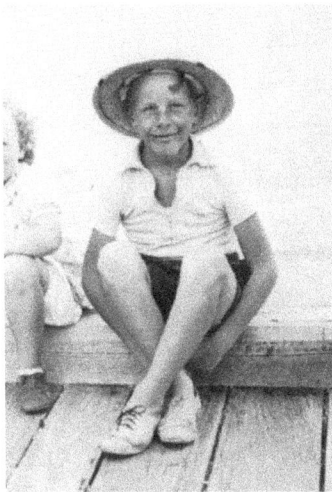

Brooks aged 7, Jervis Bay (Summer 1941)

It was early summer of 2018 when I was having coffee with my sister Sally in Wahroonga village, near where we both lived. She was eighty-one and I was eighty-five. Sally had walked to the café where we were meeting from her apartment near Abbotsleigh using her walker. I had driven.

We spoke about our children, our grandchildren and how they were all doing. We also discussed our own childhoods. We both recognized that while we, and our sister Robin, shared a common family background, our childhoods were somewhat unique to each of us given our age differences.

Then as Sally took a sip of coffee, she said, "You were born in 1933 when the horse and cart were still used. It was only after the war in 1945 that new technology came in. You lived through this period of transition; you must write your life story."

So, this chapter is the story of my early life and the times in which we lived.

Peg and Robert on their wedding day, Cambridge, MA (1932)

Our Father, Robert Christian Wilson, was born in Mudgee, NSW in 1896. He was 6 feet 2 inches (188 cm) tall with a strong athletic build, red hair and a moustache. He left school at fifteen so he could help his father on their farm. He also served with the Light Horse in Palestine during World War 1. He was well read and self-educated. His job, at the time of his marriage, and for the rest of his working life, was running the Graziers Co-operative Shearing Company (Grazcos). This was a highly respected company that at its peak shore eight million sheep per year and also had a major business in wool blending. He was knighted in 1966 for his services to Rural Australia.

Our mother, Gertrude Brooks Wilson was born in Cambridge, Massachusetts in 1901. She was a graduate of Radcliffe College (now part of Harvard). This was an interesting experience for her and one that most women of her generation did not get. She subsequently attended a summer school at the Sorbonne in Paris. My mother was around 5 feet 10 inches (178 cm) tall, attractive with black wavy hair. She was a great communicator and good tennis player.

Our parents met playing deck tennis on board a ship travelling from the United Kingdom to New York in 1929. My father asked her name. She told him to guess. He said "Peg". She said "yes". Of course, that wasn't her name. She had been christened "Gertrude" after her mother's twin sister, a name she didn't like. Rob called her Peg for the rest of her life. They were married in Cambridge, Massachusetts at our mother's parents' home on 7 May 1932. After the wedding they came to Sydney which became their home.

I was born on 30 March 1933 in the family home at 27 Bushlands Avenue, in the Sydney suburb of Gordon. Dr Angus Murray was in attendance, and it is said I was born on the kitchen table.

Following a common American tradition, I was given my mother's maiden name of Brooks as my first name. For many years I found it difficult to have such a strange first name and I used to say my name was Bruce. I'm now pleased to accept my name because it's who I am.

My sister, Sally, was born in 1937 and my sister, Robin, in 1942.

My childhood was a happy experience. I was well cared for and looked after.

Brooks (aged 3) with his mother (1936)

My father taught me to box at an early age. This was his way of playing with me and at the same time it was his way of teaching me a skill. I was taught not to fight and only to use boxing as self-defence.

Rob giving Brooks a boxing lesson, Gordon (1938 circa)

Another early memory is helping my parents water the garden with a child's watering can during a drought.

Our house was on a half-acre block which by today's standards is large. The house, vegetable garden, tool shed, and garage were in the front half. The back half was basically all bush with trees and rocks. In this area we had a fowl house and after I turned eight it was my job to feed the fowls and collect the eggs.

My father also had a black wool sheep called Blackie which he kept in the same area. I remember him bringing home shearing equipment and shearing Blackie with neighbours looking on.

Robert shearing 'Blackie' in the front yard, 27 Bushlands Ave, Gordon (1936 circa)

We also had a Dalmatian dog called Coacher. My parents gave him this name, they said, because in the old days Dalmatian dogs used to follow coaches. They were trained to attack the horses of highwaymen, thus providing protection for their owners.

Brooks with 'Coacher', the family dog, Bushlands Ave Gordon (1942 circa)

Our household domestic arrangements worked smoothly. We had a live-in maid called Lilla who did most of the cooking. We would have dinner in the dining room with Lilla waiting on the table. My mother would ring a small bell when it was time for Lilla to bring the next course. This is a level of service we don't have today.

In other areas of household management, what we had was antiquated by today's standards. We had no in-house washing machine or clothes dryer. Our laundry was a separate building at the rear of the house with a tub for boiling clothes, heated by a wood fire, and a hand ringer for squeezing out the water. Clothes dried on a clothes line in the sun. The 1930s was a period of world-wide economic depression and I remember men going door to door selling clothes props to hold up the line.

Houses also had no central heating. In the winter we kept our living room warm by having a coke-burning Esse stove. The rest of the house was very cold at night, and we frequently had colds.

Milk and bread were delivered by horse and cart. We left a billy-can by the front gate to be filled up with milk. Some people had electric refrigerators; many had ice-boxes with a man bringing a new block of ice every few days. Some people had cars, (we did), but many didn't. Most adults who worked in the city, and children who went to school, walked to and from the train station and this was a good way to know our neighbours.

The only household amenities we had were electricity, a gas stove, gas hot water, a table phone and a radio. There was no TV. Our landline telephone had automatic dialling in the same city only. To phone outside involved going through an operator.

It was only after the war that we started to move into the modern age.

For example, black and white TV came to Australia in 1956, jet aircraft travel stated in 1959, colour TV in 1975. Laptop computers became popular from 2005, and the iPhone came in 2007. Gas fired central heating became available in 1980 after a major gas pipeline was installed from Central Australia in 1972.

Childhood Highlights

My best friend, growing up, was David Patten, who lived directly across the street. He was three months older. We saw each other frequently. Our signal to meet was to let the phone ring once. After leaving school, David had a successful legal career, first as a Solicitor and then as a Judge. We are now in our late 80's and are still in touch.

Having an American mother and an Australian father opened my eyes to both countries from an early age. As a very young child I remember my mother reading me stories about "The Old Gas Lamp Lighter" who lit the gas lights in American streets. This must have been a story from her own childhood.

I also knew my father had served in the Light Horse in Palestine during World War 1 as the veranda, where I slept, had artifacts on the wall that he had collected in Egypt. I particularly remember a long piece of material attached to the wall that had pictures of Pyramids.

Christmas was a special time for me and my family, and something I looked forward to. The first Christmas I remember was when I was four. It was the morning of Christmas Eve. My father said to me "Let's go down the street to get a Christmas tree". He lifted me up on his shoulders and walked down the street to the bush below. He cut a branch off a she-oak which he carried back to our house. The tree was placed in a bucket in the living room and decorated.

Christmas Eve was also when we had our Christmas dinner, (not Christmas Day). We would join up with Uncle Hal (my father's brother), his Russian born wife, Aunt Helen, and their boys Peter and Michael. We would meet one year at our place and the next year at theirs.

During World War II we had to stop having Christmas Eve dinners together as Uncle Hal had become an army doctor and was sent to New Guinea. His family moved to the country town of Orange where it was considered safer from a possible Japanese invasion. When the war ended in 1945 Uncle Hal and his family moved back to Sydney and lived near us in Gordon. From this point on our Christmas Eve dinners together resumed.

Christmas Eve Dinner
Back row L-R: Hal (uncle), Peter (cousin), Rob (father), Chris (Grandfather), Michael (cousin)
Front row L-R: Sally (sister), "JD" - Just Dog (family dog), Peg (mother), Madam Panoff
(Hal's wife's Russian mother), Helen (aunt), Bushlands Ave, Gordon (1957 circa)

Another Christmas Eve ritual was for our parents to read us the Christmas story, "The Night Before Christmas" just before bed. Then early Christmas morning we would assemble outside our living room closed door, hoping that Santa Clause had left presents under the tree. Our father would go in first, with his eyes covered, so he couldn't see if there were any presents, (so he said), before we went in. He would turn on the Christmas tree lights, come back to us, and then we would all go in together. What joy! Santa had come!!

Christian education was part of my upbringing. When my parents tucked me into bed every night, I would say the Lord's Prayer. I also attended Sunday School at St David's Presbyterian Church in Lindfield. My Sunday School teacher was Ian Sinclair who later became a leading Australian Politician.

Several times a year we visited my father's parents (our grandparents) on their farm, "Mount Desmond". This property became an important part of my life right up to the time I left school.

Mount Desmond was 6.5 kms from Blayney on the Browns Creek Road, which was then unpaved. Blayney is west of the Blue Mountains and not far from Bathurst. It is very hot in summer and very cold in winter with strong winds. Many people call it "Chill Blayney".

Driving there took five hours during the war as petrol was rationed and we had a charcoal burner on the back to power the car. Every few hours more charcoal had to be added. We also used to stop just over the Blue Mountains at Little Hartley and have tea and scones. We would also buy a bag of apples to take to the farm.

On these long drives, my father from time to time spoke about his experience in Palestine during World War I. He said there were long periods of boredom when nothing was happening. Then there were short periods of intense fear during a battle. He said when this happened men would stop swearing as they did not want to die with a swear word on their lips.

As we travelled along, other drivers would give us a wave and my father would speak about being in the "friendly country". This was how country people related at that time.

Brooks (aged 5) and Ron Johnston; Mount Desmond (1938)

Mount Desmond was 800 acres. It had steep hills and valleys with a creek running through the middle. There were trees scattered throughout in sufficient quantity to provide firewood for the house. It was sheep country with grass and clover paddocks. Income came from selling fat lambs and wool.

All stock work was with horses, including a draft horse called Prince. My mother had a horse called Mary Lou. Mine was Teddy, named after Edward (or Teddy) Duke of Windsor, who had abdicated as King. Sally was given a horse called Tony.

Mother with Sally; Mount Desmond, NSW (1939)

The only machinery on the farm was my grandfather's Model T Ford which was started by using a crank handle in the front. He had placed leather binding around the steering wheel as his way of looking after" Lizzie" as he called his car.

The house on the farm was 200m from the front gate, on top of a fairly steep hill. It had commanding views of the farm land below and the road leading into Blayney. There were tall pine trees along the driveway leading up to the house with the sweet smell of pine needles and the sound of birds singing. There was a hedge and flower garden in front of the house.

The house, itself, was made of wood, the only bricks being the chimney and large fireplace inside. All rain falling on the roof was collected in a large tank. There was no town water or electricity. Internal lighting was by kerosene lamp. Cooking was on a wood fired stove. The toilet was a deep hole in the ground in a separate building at the back.

Even though the house was rudimentary, the meals we had were delicious. I remember roast lamb and bread-and-butter pudding. The wood fired stove could produce whatever an electric stove does today.

In winter, the wind would howl around the house. The main living room, with kitchen, dining table, lounge chairs and radio, was warm due to logs burning in the large fireplace. The rest of the house was freezing.

Mail was delivered three times a week. I loved to stand in front of the house around mid-day looking down to the main road. Way off to the right I could see a horse and sulky coming around the bend. It was the mailman.

As I grew older, I would spend school holidays at Mount Desmond, travelling there by steam train. Sally would sometimes come too. The farm manager would meet us at Blayney Railway Station and take us by horse and sulky to the farm. This was about a 45-minute trip.

Brooks with granddaughters Emma and Louisa during a weekend visit with John and Sue's family; Blayney Railway Station (2019)

Typical horse and sulky, similar to Blayney (1935 circa)

The farm manager lived on the farm with his wife. (My grandparents had retired and moved into Blayney). There was Harry Davidson initially and then Alec Deane. Mr. Deane (as I called him) had been in the Light Horse in Palestine during World War 1, the same as my father. I often heard the two men exchanging war stories.

One of the war stories they spoke about was the battle of Romani (pronounced Ro-mar-nee) in Palestine held between 3-5 August 1916. Romani was in the Sinai Desert not far from the Suez Canal. The Australian Light Horse successfully stopped the Turkish advance at this point. It was difficult country with deep sand that made it hard to walk and it was also extremely hot.

Australian camp outside Romani showing covered horse stable
and protective barbed wire (Wikipedia) (1916 circa)

Light Horse Heading out on Patrol (Wikipedia); Palestine (1916)

Alec Deane had been in this battle. My father arrived the day after it ended. It was the first time he had seen dead bodies on the ground.

Living and working on the farm was a great experience for me. I was taught how to milk a cow, muster sheep, help with the shearing and catch rabbits who were in plague proportions. Catching rabbits involved taking dogs who would either catch them or chase them into burrows. Pulling a rabbit out of a burrow was a tricky business. It involved putting a stick into the burrow to ensure there was no snake there. If the point of the stick had fur on it when withdrawn, it was safe to pull the rabbit out. The next step was to kill the rabbit and skin it. At age twelve the first money I ever earned was through selling rabbit skins to a dealer in Blayney.

Robert, my grandfather Chris, and Fred Gorman holding dead rabbits;
Mount Desmond (1931)

I liked life on the farm so much that at age fourteen I told people I was planning to be a farmer when I left school. My plans changed after the farm was sold when I was fifteen and I turned my sights to a university education.

Brooks, aged 15; Mount Desmond (1948)

In mid-1938 my mother's parents, Clayton and Grace Brooks, came to visit. They had left Boston by train and travelled across the country to San Francisco. Then they boarded the "Mariposa" and sailed to Sydney. Total journey time was about 3 weeks.

It was exciting to have them arrive. My mother had not seen her parents since 1935 when she had taken me to the United States to show off her son. (I have no memory of this visit).

It was also exciting for me to have my American grandparents with us. My grandfather gave me my first watch and my first Bible that I still have.

A family photo was taken outside our garage. It includes both sets of grandparents, my mother and father and my baby sister Sally sitting on my father's shoulders. I was the proud little boy standing in the front. After the photo was taken, I remember running as fast as I could up the path to our house. This was my way of expressing delight at what was happening.

(L-R: Grace Brooks (grandmother), Mary Wilson (grandmother) , Peg (mother), Chris Wilson (grandfather), Clayton Brooks (grandfather). Rob (father) is peering through the back with Sally (sister) on his shoulders. The small boy in front is Brooks Wilson); Bushlands Ave, Gordon.

In the summer we would go on beach holidays. I particularly remember Jervis Bay with its crystal-clear water and white sand. Other families we knew would go there too, so there were lots of kids to hang out with.

Brooks on far right with family friends; Jarvis Bay (1941)

Rob and Peg with Brooks (far left) and Sally and other family friends; Jarvis Bay (1941)

On September 1, 1939, World War 11 was declared. I was six. I remember being in the car with my mother as she parked in the garage at home. It was late afternoon, and I asked my mother why the church bells were ringing. She replied that England was at war with Germany and as a member of the British Empire, Australia was at war too. The United States was not involved. Knowing my mother was American I asked: "What side would you be on if England and the US were at war?" "It couldn't happen," was her reply.

The American policy of neutrality changed on December 7, 1941, when Japan bombed Pearl Harbor. The United States declared war on Japan. As a result, Australia became a staging ground for one million troops who passed through here on their way to fight the Japanese. We had soldiers my mother had known in Boston come and visit us. This included General Macarthur's secretary, Colonel Larry Bunker.

Australian troops were also involved. In early 1941 troops from the 8th Australian Division were sent to Singapore to protect the island from a possible Japanese attack. When the attack did come in early 1942 the Japanese overcame the Australian defences and captured Singapore on February 15, 1942. The Australian troops became prisoners of war. This included Ron Johnston who had grown up in Manly and had lived and worked at Mount Desmond before the war. I liked Ron very much as he let me work with him. On one of my visits, I heard him say to Thora, the young lady who cooked our meals, "After the war I hope to join the Fire Brigade." He never did. He died as a prisoner of war on the Burma Railway.

In March 1942, my mother told me she was going to have a baby. I remember hearing this as she lay resting on her bed after I had come home from school.

Then, on the night of May 31, 1942, Japanese midget submarines entered Sydney Harbour. Their target was an American cruiser which they missed and sank a ferry instead. Twenty-one people died. The submarines were destroyed and later one was put on display in the Domain. I was taken to see it by my father's secretary, Helen Davis.

Robbie was born on June 4, four days after the Japanese attack, The nurse who had come when Sally was born, Sister Burton, came again and stayed a week. She was followed by Valerie Wass who stayed longer.

Japanese Submarine (from Google); Sydney Harbour (1942)

My other memories of the war include listening to war news on the radio, rationing of petrol, sugar and clothing, and air raid precautions. We had slit trenches at school, all streets had air raid sirens installed and houses had blackout blinds to prevent light seeping out. Sydney beaches had barbed wire along the whole beach to make a possible landing by the Japanese more difficult.

The War in the Pacific ended on September 1, 1945, when the Japanese surrendered. I was twelve years old.

General Macarthur accepts Japanese surrender from Japanese Foreign Minister
Mamoru Shigemitsu (Google); on the deck of USS Missouri (September 1945)

My early life was a very happy experience. I had parents who loved me, they gave me a great education and they taught me how to live by their example. It was their influence that became the key to my life.

My father taught me a great deal just through who he was. As mentioned previously he had grown up on a farm which required hard work and knowing the value of money as there was no surplus cash. He was very practical. Despite leaving school at fifteen he was well read and self-educated. He was a good listener who could also articulate what he thought clearly. He was a hard worker, both in his job and at home where he maintained the garden, fixed broken things and actively helped my mother. He had good values and often spoke about doing the right thing and helping others. He taught me good table manners and how to relate to others. He told me if you can't say something nice about someone, don't say anything. He was a good maths teacher and helped me with math homework. A highlight of my time with him was when he took me camping when I was around twelve. It was just the two of us. He set up the tent and cooked dinner.

After we were both in bed we chattered before going to sleep. I asked him "How old were you when you got married?" He replied "Thirty-six". I asked "Why did you wait so long? He said that he didn't know.

Next morning when we woke up, he said there was something he wanted to tell me as he didn't want to keep secrets from his son. He said the reason he was thirty-six when he married my mother was because he had been married before.

I asked him what had happened. He said his first wife didn't like being married. She was a doctor and was now living in England. He said that he had always thought a marriage break up would never happen to him as he was not a womanizer and he lived by a strict moral code.

But the break up did happen. He asked me not to tell anyone as he didn't want my sisters to know, So I didn't tell anyone until long after his death when I found out that most people knew.

My final comment about growing up concerns my mother. She knew the value of education. She helped me study and it was her influence that led me to Sydney University and ultimately to Harvard Business School. This education opened the door to my subsequent career.

In 1955 I was twenty-two when I left home to go to the United States. I returned in 1959 at age twenty-six with a wife.

I was now in a new phase of my life.

Additional Chapter 1 Photos:

Robert & Brooks (1935 circa)

My Family of Origin
L-R: Brooks (aged 22), Sally, Robyn, Robert, Gertrude (1955)

Rethers' home playing tennis with Peg, Robert & Brooks; Wahroonga (1942 circa)

Brooks & Robbie; Bushlands Ave, Gordon (1945)

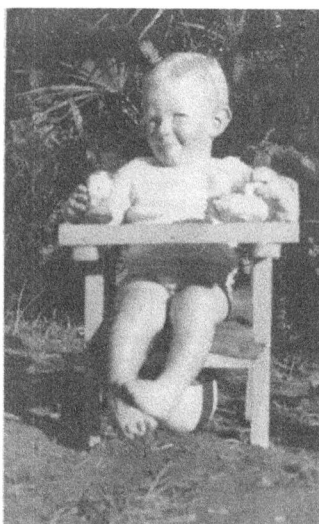

BCW photo sent to Aunt Barbara (Peg's sister) in USA; Bushlands Ave, Gordon (1934 circa)

Visiting cometary (l to r) Ann, Sue, Emma, Louisa, Peter Wilson,
Brooks, Lyn (John taking photo); Blayney NSW (2018)

~ CHAPTER 2 ~

School Days

Brooks (in Killara uniform) and Sally; Gordon (1941 circa)

The first school I went to was Killara Preparatory School, located in Arnold Street, Killara. (The school no longer exists). I was 4 years old and it was 1937. My mother used to drive me there every day and pick me up.

There must have been 100 boys at the school. Mr Chapman was Headmaster and owner of the school. He had previously been a teacher at Knox. He had little contact with the boys and all I remember about him is that he used to read us stories from Charles Dickens. There was also a Miss Perrin.

We all wore school uniforms and played marbles during our breaks. I had a bag of marbles I carried with me.

Killara Preparatory School photo (Brooks is in center, 3rd row up, leaning in behind the post) (1940 circa)

I also remember going swimming in the Olympic Pool in North Sydney with my class. I was a poor swimmer and a bigger boy tried to dunk me. I offered him an ice cream if he didn't do this. He accepted.

After three years at Killara Prep, I spent one year at Gordon Public School and then went to Knox.

I first became aware of Knox in late 1941 when I was 8 years old. One evening in November my father said to me "we're sending you to Knox next year and tonight we are going to meet the Master-in-Charge, Mr. Haslett." So, my father cut my finger nails and made me presentable and the two of us went to Ewan House. It was in the evening. We entered the vestibule at Ewan House and announced who we were. Mr Tom Haslett came down from upstairs where he lived. We stood in the vestibule talking for about 5 minutes and at the end of the interview I was accepted for Knox.

Next year, in 1942, I started at Knox. I was in form 3. Our class Master was Mr. Coite, or "Coitie" as the boys called him. There was also a Mr Morrow and a Miss Stowe. Miss Stowe was still there when my own sons attended the Prep School many years later.

Mr Haslett had been a Christian Missionary in China before the war. He was a great gentleman and I remember him saying that the new millennium would be in 2000 and that we boys would see it but that he wouldn't be around. This was perhaps the first time I thought about death.

Mrs. Haslett was also a great inspiration. She was Swiss and a very fine lady. On my final year in the Prep School, I was given the role of a girl called Barbara Allen in the school play. Mrs. Haslett taught me how to sing and play the tune of Barbara Allen on the piano. This is still the only tune I know how to play.

An interesting aspect of my playing a girl is that I was wearing one of my mother's dresses. Before our form went onto the stage to perform, we stood in the back of the darkened hall waiting for the previous class to finish. As I was standing there one of the fathers came up to me and offered me a seat. I wondered why? I then realized he thought I was a girl. So, my mother's dress worked well.

Some of the things I remember from the Prep School are air-raid drills when we had to go outside and get into a fairly deep trench. I also remember clothes rationing during the war and the special coupons that were needed to buy clothes. I also remember scoring my first try in rugby.

At the beginning of 1945 I went to the Senior School. I was 11 years old. The war against Japan ended that September. I still remember the excitement that everyone felt. I left Knox 5 years later in 1949 at the age of 16 after completing the Leaving Certificate and qualifying to enter Sydney University.

The Senior School was a great experience especially with the influence of older boys. I remember Rex Godfrey who taught me lifesaving and Ian Sinclair who had been my Sunday School teacher and was School Captain.

The teachers who made the greatest impression on me were:

The Headmaster, Dr Bryden, who laid down strict rules and was respected by the boys.

Dr Fahey, who taught Maths. He was Irish and an inspiring teacher who drove the boys hard. He carried a small fan belt around with him which he used to whack the boys to make them pay attention. I learnt a lot from him.

H.G. Shaw was another inspiring teacher who taught French. He had been in the Air Force during the war and at the end of the war I still remember him coming to school in his uniform. H.G. Shaw was very much a gentleman and a very enthusiastic teacher. I also owe a lot to him. In one particular year, thanks to his teaching and my mother's coaching, I was able to share the French prize with fellow student Alan Batley.

Allan Briggs was the best all-round teacher I ever ha d. He was a great athlete and could drop kick a football over the goal posts from a most oblique angle. He also led cadets and he taught English. I got from him a love of Shakespeare and I still think of him as a very inspiring human being. I owe a lot to him. For the Leaving Certificate in 1949 we had to study Macbeth. I also read Julius Caesar. Now, 72 years later, I still remember lines from Julius Caesar:

> *His life was gentle*
> *And the elements in him so mixed*
> *That Nature might stand up and say to all the world*
> *This was a man.*
>
> —W. Shakespeare ('Julius Caesar')

I wrote to Allan Briggs a few weeks before he died and told him he was the best teacher I ever had. I was glad I did this.

Allan Briggs wrote back thanking me for the letter.

While most of the teachers were inspiring, there were some who could not keep order. I remember one teacher who would spend a lot of time writing on the board with his back turned to the class. When this happened boys would throw oranges at each other around the room. On one occasion an orange went out the window. When the teacher turned around the boy who threw it put up his hand and asked if he could be excused to go to the toilet. He was given permission. He went outside, picked up the orange and threw it back through the window. He then came back in. The teacher made no comment.

Apart from studies, Knox provided great training in various sporting activities, including boxing which I did in my early years. We were taught by a Mr Taylor who also handed out lollies.

I remember boxing a 3-minute Round with another boy which was very hard work. I was also taught that if you ever wanted to hit someone in self-defense, the best place to hit them was on the side of their jaw.

I only had to use this technique once. We were at a cadet camp some years later and we were standing outside our huts at the end of the day. In a sky larking fashion, a boy grabbed hold of my left hand and pulled my thumb back as hard as he could. This was very painful and I told him to stop. He did. I also said if you do it again, I'll hit you. He did do it again so I hit him in the jaw as I had been taught. He fell to the ground and they had to carry him inside. Fortunately, he was not badly hurt and soon recovered. For my part. I didn't have any more trouble.

Team work and leadership were also key things we were taught at Knox. We had House drilling every morning on the oval at recess. We were in sections of 6 or 8 and one of the boys had to give military type orders as we were marching around. In this way many boys learnt the art of taking orders as well as giving orders. Our aim was to win the drill competition. I don't recall if we ever did.

Cadets was a logical extension of this and this was even better training. I sat for promotion exams as soon as I could and was a Corporal one year and a Cadet Officer the next.

CADET OFFICERS.

Back Row: Ahern, D. G.; McGee, R. G.; Latimer, C. D.; Jones, S. B.
Front Row: Wilson, B. C.; Pratt, F. W.; A. W. Briggs, Esq. (Capt.); Dingle, A. F.; Graham, W. J.

The 1949 Knox Cadet Officers

One of my good friends both at school and in the cadets, was Tony Dingle (front row, second from the right) who had come with his parents from the UK. After graduating from Sydney University Tony joined the Australian Diplomatic Corps. At the end of his career, he retired to the UK. Some 15 years ago he contacted me to say he had cancer. He died shortly after. I was pleased to hear from him.

Apart from cadets, Sport was another great learning experience.

In 1949 I represented the school in the First XV Rugby. I was Lock.

The first competitive game we played that year was against Waverly, the premier rugby school in our competition. We won! Unbelievable... Unfortunately, in all subsequent games against other schools, we lost. Such is life.

Knox Grammar 1st XV 1949 (Brooks seated on right)

In athletics I was the High Jump champion in 1948 and 1949. The technique we all used at that time was known as "scissors". This involved going over the bar legs first rather than head and back first which is the technique used now.

The Knox Athletics Team (1948)

In our final year, senior boys were given positions of authority to ensure younger boys followed School Rules. Those who broke rules came before the committee and could be caned by a Prefect. I am sure this practice of caning has long since stopped.

School Photo of Prefects and Probationers (1949)

So, to summarize, Knox taught me to work hard to achieve my academic goals and also my extracurricular goals.

This was great training for life as nothing in life comes automatically. We live in a competitive world and each achievement has to be earned.

I was also taught to do the manly thing, (Virile Agitur is the school moto). To me, this meant treating all people with respect and being honest and trustworthy. I have tried to live by these rules all my life.

In looking back over my own life and what I have done, I owe a great deal to Knox. It was training at Knox that enabled me to become an Officer in the Sydney University Regiment at the age of 18 and also helped me become a company Managing Director at the age of 37.

Other Photos

Robbie and Brooks; Gordon (1943 circa)

CHAPTER 3

Sydney University

Sydney University (Google) (2021)

W hen I left school in December 1949, I had no idea what I wanted to do. I asked my parents what they thought. My mother's strong advice was to "seek further education". She had gone to Radcliffe College (now part of Harvard) when she had left school and gained a Bachelor of Arts Degree. This had given her more knowledge of the world and greater maturity. She felt a similar experience would do the same for me. Additionally, she thought that going as a full-time day student, as opposed to just night classes and a daytime job, was the best option. Her view was that a major part of the learning experience was meeting other students and being involved in student activities.

How right she was.

So, I took my mother's advice and decided to go to Sydney University. But what should I study? I knew I didn't want to do Law, Medicine, or Vet Science, so I enrolled in the Faculty of Arts to get a general education. I lived at home and was a Day student.

In my first year I studied English, Philosophy, Ancient History and Economics. Of these, Philosophy was the subject I found the most interesting as we studied the Socratic Dialogues.

In my second year I transferred to the Faculty of Economics as my father felt an Economics Degree would be better training for an ultimate business career. So, I did this and three years later graduated as Bachelor of Economics.

Sydney Uni. graduation (Brooks, second from left, with friends) (1953)

What did I learn in getting this Degree? I learnt how to think and write more clearly and do research. I also got to know about previous economic thinkers, starting with Adam Smith who wrote "The Wealth of Nations" in 1776.

However, the main things I learnt came from student activities. This included the Sydney University Regiment and the Sydney University Liberal Party Branch. Both these groups taught me a great deal about life and were major factors in shaping my future career.

I will write about the Sydney University Regiment first.

My initial week at the University in early March 1950 was "Freshers Week". This is the time when student clubs and groups recruit new members. The Sydney University Regiment (SUR) was one of these groups. I had been involved with the cadets at Knox so joining the SUR was a logical extension of this.

The problem was that to join the Citizen Military Forces (of which the SUR was part), you had to be eighteen. I was only sixteen at that time but about to turn seventeen on March 30. So, I put my age up a year and joined. This was a good time to join as the Korean war had started and Australian forces were involved. It was possible that men my age would be conscripted and if this happened it would be better if I had some kind of rank.

So, the SUR became my main extra-curricular activity. I went to camps, studied to become a Non-Commissioned Officer (NCO) and then a Lieutenant in 1951.

The reason I had been promoted so quickly was there had been a large influx of students into the Regiment due to the Korean War. People who could take a leadership role were needed and I was there at the right time.

Being an officer was great training in leadership. I was a Platoon commander which meant I had to train my men in marching, weapon handling and night-time manoeuvres which included digging foxholes. In conducting this task, it was my job to look after my men. This included ensuring they had their meals before I had mine.

After graduating from Sydney University in 1953, I transferred to the University of NSW Regiment and was promoted Captain. This meant I was now in charge of a Company which was made up of three platoons. I served there until I went to the United States in 1955.

My military experience did not end then. It started up again when I was working in New York for eighteen months after Harvard Business School. I had myself attached to the 42nd Infantry Division of the National Guard in New York City. I wore my Australian Army Uniform and was made Assistant-Aid to the General.

General Nast says "farewell" to Brooks; New York City (1958)

This was a most interesting experience. It involved weekly parades and a week-long camp at Camp Drum in upstate New York. I participated in firing shells from a tank and flying with a pilot in a small military plane at night for artillery spotting drills. The plane followed the roads and would climb steeply as cars just below us were spotted. I also met the Governor of New York, Averill Harriman, who visited the camp. He told me he had met the Australian Prime Minister Robert Menzies during World War II in London.

A humorous event occurred some months later when I was walking along a street in New York in my Australian Army Uniform. An American soldier who was coming towards me gave me a salute and I saluted back. After we had both gone on a few paces he called out "What army uniform are you wearing?"

My military career ended when I returned to Australia in 1959 with my wife Ann and we lived in Mount Isa. There was no army unit there and, in any case, I was entering a new phase of my life.

In looking back at this military experience, it taught me what it takes to be a leader. This was a valuable lesson as it helped me in my subsequent career running a company as will be explained later.

Turning now to my second main interest in student activities - my involvement with the Sydney University Liberal Party Branch.

1950 was an interesting time in Australian politics. Menzies had won the election on 10 December 1949 against a left-wing Labor Party that wanted to nationalize the banks.

There was also an active communist element within the Trade Union movement that aimed to end the current economic system.

In 1951 Menzies introduced a law to ban the Communist Party of Australia and he arranged for a referendum to be held on this. At that time, I was President of the Sydney University Liberal Party Branch and I invited former Prime Minister Billy Hughes to give a lunchtime talk at the University in support of the Menzies legislation. Part of the arrangement was that I was to collect Billy Hughes at his house in Lindfield and return him home after his talk. I had a hire car so I could speak with the former Prime Minister without having to worry about driving. He turned out to be a most affable person who could listen as well as talk.

When we got to the University, we met his secretary who was waiting. As we moved onto the stage, he asked her to please whisper in his ear, while he was talking, if there was anything else he should say. Towards the end of his talk, I thought of something else he might want to say and suggested this to his secretary. She went forward and whispered in his ear as had been arranged. He immediately said, "I have been reminded to say something I had forgotten...My secretary would make a good wife." I don't know if women would like this said about them today, but I'm sure Billy meant it as a compliment. He then went on to discuss the additional point that I had suggested.

Many other interesting politicians came to speak. This included Prime Minister Robert Menzies, future Governor General Paul Hasluck, and future Prime Minister Harold Holt. Meeting these people in my early life gave me the confidence to reach out to similar important people in later years.

Being President of the Liberal Party Branch also got me close to the Student Union newspaper "Honi Soit", which is still in circulation today. The challenge here was to get our stories published.

I remember how we did this once when there was a key issue that we wanted publicized. One of our members was Peter Tranter who wrote frequently for the student newspaper. At our request he wrote a story about the outcome of one of our meetings before we even had the meeting. His story was published.

Apart from time spent at the University itself, I had a variety of jobs during the long summer vacations which gave me experience in different industries and broader knowledge of the world. My first two summer jobs were in Sydney and the last two were in Central Australia and in Port Moresby.

- In the summer of 1950-51, I had a labouring job with Ku-ring-gai Council digging ditches. We used picks and shovels and had no mechanical equipment. Any material we needed, such as sand, was brought to us by a horse and cart. I liked the hard physical work and I also enjoyed being with men whose whole career was doing what I was doing.

- In the summer of 1951-52, I had an engine repair job in a car factory in Sydney. My job was to help fix car engines, working with a man who knew what he was doing. My father had arranged this job as he wanted me to learn how to fix my own car if I broke down in the Outback. The job I had was valuable experience, but I didn't learn enough to fix my car.

- In the summer of 1952-53 I had a job on a cattle station called "Helen Springs", 96kms north of Tennant Creek and over 10,000 square km in area. In getting there I flew into Tennant Creek and took the airport bus to the hotel to meet Eric Nicholson, the Helen Springs manager, who had come in to meet me. I had an interesting experience after we met. Eric took me into the bar to buy me a beer. He also offered one to the bartender behind the bar. The bartender said that he was not allowed to drink behind the bar, so he came around to the customer side and had his drink. He then returned to his side. He had followed the letter of the law in a way that was probably not intended.

Helen Springs, Northern Territory (Google)

I enjoyed my time at Helen Springs. It was a scorching summer in the middle of a drought. My job was to drive around with Bill Kelly who was responsible for fixing windmills used for pumping artesian water into troughs for the cattle to drink. Bill and I often had to sleep on the ground near one of the windmills, so we always had our swags with us. Bill taught me how to climb to the top of a windmill and feel safe in doing this... Because there had been a long drought, all the grass around the water troughs had been eaten and the cattle had to walk in long distances from where they had grass to have a drink. There was no shade around the troughs and after drinking a great deal of water the cattle would bloat and be unable to move. Part of our job was to hit them on the head with an axe to put them out of their misery.

This was also my first experience of meeting Aboriginals. I met a young man my age who taught me how to throw boomerangs and spears. On another occasion I was driving along with Bill Kelly in our truck. We had an Aboriginal man, Mick, on the tray at the back. Suddenly there was banging on the roof. Mick asked us to stop. He had seen a goanna lizard. Jumping down, he grabbed it. "Good tucker" he said. Mick also had a "Bull Roarer" around his neck which was a thin piece of wood on a string. When taken off his neck and twirled around it made a "bull roaring" sound. Mick said the purpose of this was to "call him up rain."

Helen Springs was very isolated at the time I was there. We had no phone or radio and had no idea what was happening in the outside world. There must have been newspapers that were flown to Tennant Creek and possibly delivered to Helen Springs, but I didn't see them.

Brooks showing grandchildren how to throw a spear during an extended family vacation; Central Australia (2016)

In the summer of 1953-54, I had a job working in Port Moresby, Papua New Guinea, with the Department of Agriculture, Stock and Fisheries. (PNG at that time was a Protectorate of Australia and under Australian control. The Australian Government arranged summer jobs for students there so they would know more about the country). I flew to Port Moresby from Rose Bay in Sydney Harbour in a Flying Boat and came back the same way.

circa Sydney Harbour: Catalina flying boat (Google) 1953

I had a routine job there working with the Supply Manager, Vince Callaghan.

Over the Christmas break a fellow student and I organized our own trek to Kokoda along the World War 11 Kokoda Trail. This is the 96km track that the Japanese soldiers had come along in 1942, hoping to capture Port Moresby. They never got there as the Australian Army stopped them. It took us 4 days to walk the trail. It was an arduous experience, up and down lofty mountains and fording rivers. There were extensive rain forests where it rained most afternoons. Young men from the native villages we came to guided us to the next village. Our payment to them was a bag of salt. Signs of the war were still there; we saw slit trenches and empty cartridge shells where there had been battles.

When we arrived in Kokoda the manager of the Plantation there invited us to stay at his place. He and his wife gave us a nice dinner and a comfortable bed. Next day we flew back to Port Moresby in a light plane then subsequently on to Sydney.

The Kokoda trip was a key experience in my life. It was something the two of us organized and implemented ourselves. We experienced the difficult terrain of the Owen Stanley Rangers and through doing this understood in greater detail what our troops had gone through eleven years previously.

Kokoda Trail, Papua New Guinea (Google)

It was now January 1954, and my student days were over. I had graduated in Economics and had learnt about life through my involvement in student activities and a variety of summer jobs that taught me about people and the challengers they faced in what they did.

It was now time to start a fulltime job. This was with the Economics Department of the Bank of NSW (now Westpac) at their Head Office in George Street, Sydney. I had no idea what this job would entail but when

I got there, I discovered it was to sit at a desk and summarize magazine articles.

This was an interesting way to start my career as it taught me that this was not the type of job I wanted. I had just walked the arduous Kokoda Trail and didn't enjoy having a passive job tied to a desk. I wanted a job where I was involved with people and creating something. So, after a year at the Bank, I knew I had to find something else.

In discussing this with various friends, two thoughts came to mind. The first was that in life we only know what we know, and it is education that lets us learn more.

The second thought was the benefits of doing the two-year Master of Business Administration (MBA) program at Harvard Business School (HBS). There were no MBA programs in Australia at that time. It was said that graduates from the Harvard program gained good jobs in industry and quickly rose to the top. This seemed the type of course I wanted.

Additional Photos

At the beach with surf kayak and friends (1951 circa)

~ CHAPTER 4 ~

Harvard Business School

Cambridge, MA: Harvard Business School (Google)

With my parent's help and support I applied to Harvard Business School (HBS) and was accepted. I had to be in the United States by September 1955 when classes started.

On my way there, I decided to visit Europe first. I left Sydney in May 1955, on the Italian ship "M.V. Sorrento". To save money I went Tourist Class and was in a cabin below deck with three other men. Despite being a Tourist passenger, I was able to spend most of my time in First Class as I helped organize activities for the passengers.

We had an interesting trip which must have lasted about a month with stops along the way. We went through the Suez Canal and eventually arrived in Naples where I left the ship.

At this point I linked up with a male passenger from New Zealand and we hitch-hiked to Paris. Along the way we stopped in Verona where there was an Opera being performed outdoors. People were sitting in the stands holding candles. It was a beautiful experience.

We eventually got to London where I stayed with my father's friend, Fred Gorman and his family. (Fred Gorman later became my Best Man when I got married in London in 1959). After time in London and hitch hiking to Scotland, I took the "Queen Mary" to New York. My mother's sister, Aunt Barbara, met me at the wharf and took me back to her home in Port Chester where I met her husband, Ted, and my cousins Bruce and David who were around my age. After a few days there we drove to the Brooks Family summer home in Paris Hill, Maine which had been an important part of my mother's life.

Cousins Bruce and David Rideout and John Brooks (from an earlier time);
Paris Hill, ME (1949)

Paris Hill, ME: View of Lake Pennesseewassee

As I discovered, Paris Hill is a unique and beautiful place. It was the county seat (capital city) before the railway was built. When the railway came, the county seat changed. Paris Hill was left as it was - elegant houses around a Common with a church in the middle. President Lincoln's first Vice President, Hannibal Hamlin, came from there as did Harry Lyon who was the navigator on Kingsford Smith's inaugural flight from America to Australia. The scenery is beautiful with the White Mountains in the background. The freshwater lakes are large and great for swimming and canoeing. The country club has a nice golf course and lobster dinners. Families from Boston, New York and Pittsburgh owned summer houses there. When I arrived in Paris Hill my grandmother, Grace Brooks, had already arrived from Boston. I felt very close to all my relatives and fully accepted as a member of the Brooks Family which I was proud to be.

Having this American background was very helpful as at no time during my time there did, I feel like a foreigner. I had grown up in Australia but having close relatives in the States made me feel very much at home there.

This close connection with the US was to become a central feature of my life. My wife, Ann, came from there and I ended up working for an American company in Australia as I will describe later. I thought of the US as my second home and still do.

In early September 1955 I started my studies at Harvard Business School.

Harvard Business School is across the Charles River from the main Harvard University. It is a short walk to Harvard Square and the town of Cambridge which is a suburb of Boston.

The institution is now over 110 years old and has a well laid out campus. The school runs a two-year Master in Business Administration (MBA) Program with around one thousand students per year. Each year is divided into sections of one hundred. I was in Section E. It also runs Advanced Management programs of shorter durations.

In my MBA program most students were in their mid-twenties. I was one of the youngest being twenty-two. Most unmarried students lived on campus with two men to a room. There were four rooms to a suite, all attached to a common bathroom.

My roommate in the second year was Leo Fortin, a French Canadian who came from Quebec. We became good friends and I visited him at his home and met his parents. He also stayed with us in Paris Hill, Maine for a few days when my mother was visiting.

Friends from an adjoining room were Charles McIntosh and Chuck Gangloff. They had been at the Naval Academy and had served in the US Navy prior to coming to HBS. Both these men became good friends and we saw a lot of each other. This included buying breakfast foods and having breakfast together in one of our rooms.

All instruction at HBS is by the Case Method. This involves students being given written business cases which they first discuss in small groups prior to attending a Section discussion. In the Section discussion the tiered classrooms have swivel chairs so we could see everyone from where we sat. The lecturers' job was to facilitate discussion, not to give his point of view.

The basic idea, therefore, was for students to teach themselves.

My best subject was Marketing. I was also taught about Finance, Human Motivation and other subjects relating to Business Management.

Students came from all over the US and, in my Section, one from each of Canada, the UK and Germany as well as me from Australia.

When I first arrived at HBS I realized how little I knew about the United States. This included the country's history and the location of the various states. I was on a swift learning curve and keen to learn about business and all aspects of US life.

During the summer vacation between the two years, I had a summer job with the H.J. Heinz Company in Pittsburgh. When this job finished the Heinz Art Department made me a cardboard sign that said "San Francisco". I used this in hitch hiking across the country.

This was my way of seeing and learning more about the country. The interstate highway system had been installed which made it possible to drive across the country non- stop. It took me four days to get across. I had a variety of rides including trucks, families in cars and lone drivers. This gave me the chance to talk to different people. I stayed at motels overnight and picked up a new ride the next day.

When I got to the Grand Canyon, I thought I better have a look at this. So, I decided to walk to the bottom of the canyon and back. It was midsummer and very hot. I didn't carry any water or food. I got to the bottom and saw a place called "Pack Saddle" where they rent horses. I didn't stop but turned around to walk back. Walking back got harder and harder due to the steepness of the climb. It was also starting to get dark. I thought to myself "not much further to go" when my legs gave out and I couldn't walk any more. So, for the last hour I had to crawl, eventually reaching the top in complete darkness. To my relief I found I could stand again and made it back to my hotel.

Typical hiking on the Grand Canyon (Google)

I learnt from this experience that I wasn't indestructible and that it is better to think ahead when doing a walk like this and at least take water and some food.

On a separate occasion, during my hitch-hiking across the country, I was walking along the road early one morning, trying to pick up a lift. A police car pulled over and the officer said to me "What's going on?" I explained that I was a student from Australia trying to see the country which was why I was hitch hiking across. He asked, "Do you have any money?" I pulled out my wallet and showed him that I did. He was satisfied with this. He wished me well and drove off.

I thought, what a nice man.

I finally arrived in San Francisco and stayed with Kate Mailliard who was a friend of my parents. I had known her from a visit she had made to Australia several years before. One of her sons, Bill, was a Member of Congress.

After a few days in San Francisco, I travelled back to Boston with a classmate, George Abernathy, who had his own car.

The second year at HBS started in September 1956. The most interesting course I did this year was the Defense Policy Seminar put on by another branch of Harvard University. This seminar group was where Henry Kissinger got his start. Interesting people spoke to us including Frank Pace who had been Secretary of the Army under President Truman. One of his jobs had been to go to Tokyo and fire General Macarthur.

In 1956 a US Presidential election was held. I had always been interested in politics, so I went to a public meeting held in the Mechanics Hall in Boston, put on by the Democrats. Former President Harry Truman spoke, then Senator Jack Kennedy who introduced "the next President of the United States, Adlai Stevenson." Loud applause. Adlai Stevenson then spoke.

At the election in November President Eisenhower won, but it was interesting for me to have been at an election rally.

At the end of the academic year there were lots of job interviews including one with the American Smelting and Refining Company who had a controlling interest in Mount Isa Mines in Australia. They were looking for people to work with them in New York for eighteen months prior to going to Mount Isa.

As I have written in Chapter 5, I did accept this job and worked in New York City. I met my future wife, Ann, there. We were married in London on 18 April 1959.

~ CHAPTER 5 ~

Marriage and Family Life

Christmas with Brooks, Ann and all their children and grandchildren; Warrawee (2010)

As I look back at my life it is my family that has given me my greatest joy. Nothing else comes close.

At the centre of this was my wife, Ann, and our sixty-one years of marriage, followed by our four children and now nine grandchildren.

It is true I had a career that I enjoyed, but the significance of this is that it gave us income that enabled us to have a comfortable home, educate our children and take the whole family on trips to various locations and countries that enriched our lives.

I will start at the beginning. After I graduated from Harvard Business School in June 1957, I worked in New York City for eighteen months. I lived with three other HBS graduates who had an apartment at 245 E 72nd Street. My particular friend there was a fellow Australian, Bill Mitchell, who had grown up in Adelaide.

I met my wife Ann through one of the men who lived in this apartment. His name was Pete Bowditch. Pete was engaged to Phebe Alexander and at their engagement party in the early summer of 1958 I met one of her work mates, Ann Meredith.

**Ann Meredith's engagement
photo from Springfield Times (1959)**

A month or so later I met Ann again at the wedding reception held in Montauk at the end of Long Island. This was about an hour's drive from New York City. After chatting with Ann for a while I asked her "How are you getting back to NYC?" She said, "I have no idea". So, she came back with me and one of my ex-classmates who had a car.

This hour-long ride gave me a chance to get to know Ann better. Not only was she tall and good looking with a nice smile, but we had similar interest on world affairs, particularly in relation to Russia and the Cold War. She also lived about two blocks away from where I lived, which meant it was easy to meet. Our interest in Russia led us to do a Russian language course together. We also had frequent movie and dinner evenings as well as day trips to different locations, including the Civil War battlefield at Gettysburg, Pennsylvania.

Ann's job was impressive. She worked for Merrill Lynch, a leading stock broking firm, as a financial writer for their magazine, "Investors Reader." Her job involved her flying around the United States interviewing company chairmen and writing stories about their companies.

One day she told me she was coming to interview our chairman, (someone I had never met), and write a story about our company, American Smelting and Refining Company.

Ann had the meeting and then wrote her story that was published. There was a photo of Mount Isa Mines (the subsidiary I was to work for) on the front cover. How incredulous was this!

On one of our early dates Ann had told me she didn't care where she lived when she got married so I took this as an indication that she might be willing to marry me.

A major step forward came at Christmas, 1958, when she invited me to her home in Springfield, Ohio, to meet her parents. I knew from this visit we had a special relationship and in meeting her parents I could see we had similar backgrounds and values. I already knew we had the same interests.

During the visit Ann took me to their family farm which was near where they lived. I enjoyed going there and meeting Charles Penrose who ran the farm. I mention this now as in later years the farm became an important part of our lives

Nothing was said, or settled, about our long-term relationship when the time came for me to leave New York by ship for London in early January 1959. Ann came to the wharf with others to see me off. I told her then I wished she were coming with me.

As soon as I arrived in London I wrote to Ann, and she wrote back. She told me she and her parents were planning to be in Europe in a month to visit her sister Cynthia, her husband, Mike and their baby daughter, Lisa, who were living in Geneva. I wrote back suggesting that she might like to come earlier and join me in a skiing trip to Zermatt in Switzerland with my classmate Peter Hamilton and his wife Gwen.

Ann accepted and came to London. After a few days there, we flew to Switzerland. It was in the evening and as we were flying over Paris, we could see the lights twinkling below. I knew Paris was the city of romance, so this seemed like a suitable time to pop the question. I asked Ann to marry me. To my great relief she accepted.

We were married in London on 18 April 1959 in the Presbyterian Church in Marlborough Place, St John's Wood. The time of the wedding was mid-afternoon. It had been raining all day, but as we were saying our vows the sun came out. We took this as a good omen.

Brooks and Ann just married; London UK (1959)

Ann's parents were there but not mine as it was too difficult for them to travel from Sydney. Ann's Maid of Honor was her sister, Cynthia. My Best Man was my Godfather, Fred Gorman, who was a retired Ship's Captain and was well known to my parents and to me. He always visited us when his ship was in Sydney. During the war he told me he had a gun on the back of his ship, which impressed me.

Fred was assisted at our wedding by my Australian friend Frank Lang who was living in London at that time getting further medical training.

Our wedding reception was held in a house, a short walk from the church, where Ann and I planned to live after our marriage. The house had been lent to us by George and Nancy Sherman who were going away for a month. Nancy had been a roommate of Ann's in New York.

Ann's father, Palmer Meredith, spoke at our reception. He had a particularly courteous manner. He said because of the wedding he felt he was not losing a daughter but gaining a son. It was nice of him to say this given that I was taking his daughter to another country. And as I explain below, he did not lose his daughter as Ann was in regular contact with her parents, who came to visit us in Australia as well as having a joint vacation with us in Fiji.

We had two honeymoons. The first was at a seaside resort, St. Mawes, in Cornwall, an exceptionally beautiful spot. I remember driving through the picturesque countryside and crossing rivers in punts before we arrived. We stayed at the Rising Sun Hotel; a place recommended by a friend in the United Kingdom.

Having grown up in Sydney I went for a swim in the ocean. Being April, the water was still freezing. I didn't stay in very long.

After Cornwall we went back to London to get ready for our second honeymoon, which was our trip to Australia.

We were lucky to have this trip as we had no surplus cash of our own. Mount Isa Mines had given us the price of two First Class airfares from London to Sydney and said we could use the money to come back to Australia any way we liked.

In drawing up our itinerary, our aim was to visit the world's trouble spots so we could get a greater understanding of the situation. We left London in mid-June and were on the road for six weeks.

After crossing the English Channel, we went by train to Berlin, Warsaw, Kiev and Moscow, spending time in each location. We then visited Yalta and Odessa, before taking a Russian ship across the Black Sea to Istanbul, Turkey. From there we flew to Beirut, New Delhi, Calcutta, and Bangkok, before finally reaching Sydney.

Amongst all the places we visited, there are two that stand out.

The first is Russia.

Russia in 1959 was at the centre of the Cold War and had just opened to allow foreign visitors. We wanted to learn about Russia and see what a Communist society was like.

The first thing we learnt when we spent time in Moscow was that Russia was a poor country. We recognized this by the people we saw in the streets who were poorly dressed and had steel teeth. There were few up-market restaurants or Department Stores. There were few cars.

We knew that private enterprise had been abolished in Russia. Communism, it seemed to us, had been a formula for maintaining poverty rather than increasing wealth. Winston Churchill called Communism "shared misery." We thought he was right.

We gained additional insights into Russia when we visited Yalta, an up-market vacation place on the north side of the Black Sea in Crimea. Yalta has fine buildings and warm weather. It is where Churchill, Roosevelt and Stalin met during World War II.

We stayed in a hotel close to the beach and frequently wore shorts and sometimes no shoes. This practice changed when we were told it was compulsory in Russia to wear shoes. We wondered why this policy existed. The only explanation we could think of was that many poor people had chosen not to wear shoes until they were forced to.

An even greater insight into Russia occurred after I took a photo of an old woman sweeping a street. A policeman appeared and asked why I was taking this photo when there were many beautiful scenes I could photograph in Russia. He explained that because a substantial number of Russian men had been killed during the war, many women had to accept jobs such as this. He then took the film from my camera. The next morning, another policeman came to our hotel and took us to the police station for questioning.

We were seated in what seemed like a court room with rows of bench seats facing the podium. There was a photo of Lenin on the wall. The person in charge told us they had developed our film and found I had taken a photo of a bridge across the Dnieper River in Kiev. (Kiev is the capital of the Ukraine, which was then under Russian control).

He then said, "Everyone knows it is forbidden to take pictures of bridges. What spy agency do you work for?"

I replied that I didn't work for any spy agency and as I didn't speak Russian, I could hardly be a spy. I explained that I had just been married and that we had come to Russia on our honeymoon to learn about the country. I then asked why it was forbidden to take photos of bridges. He explained "Russia was almost over-run twice in the living memory of many people, and we no longer take any chances."

He then let us go.

We learnt from this experience Russia's feeling of insecurity which is still a driving force in the country today.

After leaving Russia, the second place of special interest we visited was Lebanon.

The reason we went to Lebanon was to visit a Palestinian Refugee Camp which had resulted from the Israeli occupation of Palestine in 1948. We felt compassion for the people who had been displaced.

We stayed in the capital, Beirut, which was considered to be the "Paris of the East", where wealthy Arabs went for vacations. It was on the ocean, it had up-market hotels and fine dining.

The Palestinian Refugee Camp we visited was about a two-hour drive from Beirut. The Australian Department of Foreign Affairs had arranged the visit. When we arrived, we saw a whole field of tents, each one side by side. We met the former Mayor of Jaffa and sat with him outside his tent drinking coffee, which he supplied. He was a very pleasant person and spoke English well. We asked him where all of this was heading. He explained that no one in the camp wanted to move to Jordan or any other country. They were making a political statement by staying where they were. They wanted to move back to their homes which had been taken from them at gun-point when Israel was formed in 1948.

Palestinian refugee camp (Google) (1959 circa)

It is a sad reflection on the World to think that in the sixty years since we were there, the Palestinian issue has still not been resolved.

After Lebanon, our trip continued, and we finally arrived in Sydney on July 4, 1959.

My parents met us at the airport, along with my sisters Sally and Robin. Ann had brought dresses for my two sisters which they liked. My parents had also done their best to make Ann feel welcome. As an example, my father had cut the lawn around their house the day before we arrived. We were told it was raining when he did this.

We stayed with my parents for two weeks. During this time, my parents organized a cocktail party for their friends to meet Ann. We also went to the bank to borrow money so we could buy a Holden Utility (small pick-up truck) to make the trip to Mount Isa. My father guaranteed the loan.

When it came time to leave, we packed everything we had in the back of this ute. This included a double bed we had purchased. And so, we set off.

It was a long trip of three days driving along dusty roads in outback Australia. We enjoyed the scenery. Our first stop was Dubbo, where we spent the night. We then passed through Bourke and spent the night in Longreach. Next day we were in Cloncurry before finally reaching Mount Isa in the early afternoon. As we approached the town we stopped and took a photo of our first view of where we were to live.

In Mount Isa, the Mine allocated us a house at 2 Elm Street. The house was unfurnished and the water drip air conditioning system, which the previous occupant had installed, had been removed.

Our first house on Elm Street, Mt Isa

Our first task was therefore to buy furniture and install an air conditioning system as summers in Mount Isa are extremely hot with temperatures above 40 degrees C (100 degrees F).

The air conditioning system came first. We didn't know what to do so our next-door neighbour, Bill O'Brien, took over. Bill was a foreman at the Mine;

he lined up the materials we needed and installed the duct work under the house. What a neighbourly thing for him to do!

The air conditioning system helped but only marginally.

Ann took the lead in getting furniture. Most of it came from a second-hand store as we had little money. The coffee tables we placed in the lounge room were wooden fruit boxes which we painted white and stood on their ends next to two wicker chairs.

In our front yard we had mango trees which gave us fruit we both liked.

We had a dog called Roger, who was a constant companion for Ann when I was at work. He would ride around with her in the car. Unfortunately, Roger came to a sad end about six months after we got him. Someone had given him a bait that killed him.

I'm full of admiration for what Ann did. I had taken her from a leading city in the world where she was a successful financial writer and placed her in an outback mining town in Australia.

Despite the change in life style, we enjoyed our time in Mount Isa. We made friends and we went camping with them. Ann's parents came to visit and our first child, Charles was born there in the late evening of July 17, 1960.

In the hours before Charles's was born, Ann was already in hospital, and I was performing as an extra in a stage play that night. The play was "The Man Who Came to Dinner." During the interval I got a message to go straight to the hospital. I arrived just in time to see Charles emerge from his mother's womb and take his first breath. It was an exciting experience.

Ann and Charles; Mt Isa, QLD (1961 circa)

A few weeks later my parents came to visit. My father had made a special cot for Charles which was completely covered with gauze to keep the bugs out.

In early 1961 we left Mount Isa and moved to Sydney as I had taken a job with W.D. Scott, a management consulting company. Ann and Charles flew to Sydney while I drove. We lived in a rented house in Collaroy for some months prior to buying our first home at 11 Clifford Street, Gordon.

Our first house in Sydney; 11 Clifford Street, Gordon (2021)

Our next three children were born there. I was not present at any of their births as this practice was not generally followed in Sydney.

John was born on July 2, 1962, and Mary on March 15, 1965. Andrew was born on August 3, 1967. We now had four children which is what we always wanted.

Ann's mother, Bama, had come to be with us shortly before Mary was born and shared the experience with us.

When Charles was about five and John was four, I remember taking them on an early morning run around our block. As we were coming down the hill towards our house, John fell over due to road gravel and cut open his knee. I still remember this as it was the first time, I had taken the boys running.

Ann with our four young children - Charles, John, Mary, and Andrew (1975 circa)

During all this time we had a black and white English Pointer dog called Columbus. Ann had done research and found that Pointer dogs were said to be highly intelligent. We had gone to a breeder in Tamworth and acquired him as a young puppy.

Columbus helped us make our first friends. Newspapers at that time were rolled up and delivered by someone in a car who threw them over the fences of houses up and down the street. Columbus went from yard to yard collecting the papers and bringing them back to us. One of our neighbours objected and came to talk to Ann about it. Her name was Judy Goddard. She and her husband John had children the same age as ours and we all became good friends.

Our three older children at that time went to Gordon Public School. We were also involved with the Congregational Church in Killara. We liked the Minister, Mervyn Kelly, we had friends there and our children went to Sunday school.

Money was always in short supply. Having a family was expensive and my income was quite low. I remember one day getting a knock on the door. When I opened it there was a man standing there who said, "I'm from David Jones. I've come to collect the money you owe". I paid up.

The initial few years in Gordon must have been difficult for Ann, not just because of the shortage of money. I was a young man trying to get ahead and was away a lot, including frequent trips to Asia where I was helping Australian companies sell their products.

I remember on one occasion in 1962 I had been in Tokyo for 3 weeks at the Tokyo Trade Fair. Ann remained at home in Gordon with baby Charles. It must have been a very lonely period for her. She was new to Australia and had no long-term friends.

When I returned from Tokyo, Ann met me at Sydney Airport. As we drove home Charles was in a baby seat next to Ann who was driving. I was in the back. When we got to Lindfield, we stopped at the traffic lights. There was a trailer boat parked on the side of the road. Charles said, "big boat". These were the first words I heard him speak.

At that time, I did not stay long in Sydney. Two weeks later I went to Toronto, Canada, where the Canadian National Exhibition was held. I was again helping Australian companies find markets and was away for several weeks at a time.

But where was all this leading? I knew I had to find a company that I could join and, ultimately, run. Where was this company and how could I get there? I found it hard to think of anything else.

I got my answer in March 1965, when I found the job, I wanted. Chapter 8 gives the details.

Our life changed at this point. I had an interesting job which involved Australia, Asia, and the United States. We also had a better income

In 1970 we moved from Gordon to Warrawee so we could be closer to where the children went to school. Our older children, with my parent's help, were now going to Knox (Charles and John), and Mary to Abbotsleigh). Andrew was going to Aberfeldy which was also near where we lived. He subsequently went to Knox too.

To give Ann credit, she found a broken-down house at what is now 49 Cherry Street, Warrawee. Ann saw what this house could become. We bought it, had an architect, (my childhood friend Ted Rethers), draw up plans for the house and a landscape gardener designs a new garden. The house became exactly what we wanted. It has the accommodation we needed, and it also has what is now a beautiful garden and swimming pool. We have lived here for over fifty years.

Our Family home on Cherry Street (2019 circa)

During their growing up years, the children were central to our lives, and still are. We gave them our total love and support. We tried to teach them by example. This included how to treat others, the merits of working hard, having good manners and being trustworthy. We took a great interest in what they did. This included their school work, (and subsequently University work), sporting activities and outside interests.

Outside interests were different for each child. For Charles it was magic tricks; for John it was reptiles and nature; for Mary it was Duke of Edinburgh activities and for Andrew it was sailing at Crusader camps.

There were times when our children needed special care. This was particularly so in Andrew's case when he was 13 in 1981.

One night when we were all in bed, Andrew called out "I can't sleep. I have a pain in my chest". I went into his room to be with him. Ann and I both thought he was too young to have any heart problems, so I gave him some Disprin and he went back to sleep.

Next day we took him to the local doctor and finally to a heart specialist, Gaston Bauer. Gaston conducted various tests and found that Andrew's problem was a leaking heart valve. To have this fixed Gaston recommended we take Andrew to the Texas Heart Institute in Houston as operations of the type he needed were not carried out in Australia at this time.

So, this is what we did. Gaston set up appointments for us in Houston and he also arranged for our Hospital Contribution Fund to pay the cost of the surgery.

Ann and I then flew to Houston with Andrew and checked him into the hospital; we stayed in the Hilton Hotel nearby. Ann's sister Cynthia flew in to be with us.

The night before the operation I remember lying on the bed next to Andrew and saying to him " I wish I could take your place". He replied, "Don't worry; I'll be OK".

So next day he had the operation with the world-renowned surgeon Dr. Denton Cooley. Everything worked out fine. After a week we flew back to Sydney and resumed our normal lives.

Andrew's recovery was quick. He was able to return to school

How lucky we were.

In resuming our normal lives, we went camping over Easter as we did every year. This involved sleeping in the one big tent and cooking on an open fire. We all loved this experience.

On one of our camping trips, I remember teaching Andrew how to drive when he was still quite young. I was with him the first few times we went around the track. I then got out and let him go by himself. He couldn't believe it. He did fine.

(l to r) John, Charles, Ann, Andrew Mary (Brooks taking photo); Dungog, NSW (1970)

In the winter we went skiing in Perisher. On our periods of "home leave" we went back to the United States but on our way there we visited other countries including Europe, Africa, and South America.

In the summer we went to Terrigal every year. When we first went there it was about two hours from where we lived. It is now one-hour thanks to a new Expressway. We went there as our Gordon neighbours, the Goddards, suggested we might enjoy it there. They had an apartment on the beach.

Initially we rented an apartment, not always the same one. We did not particularly enjoy this experience. We often had to sleep three to a room and often the beds were most uncomfortable. So, we decided to build our own place.

In 1982 we purchased land on the beach front close to where the Goddards had their place. We built a comfortable house with four bedrooms and a large deck in front overlooking the ocean.

A painting of Terrigal Beach - The view from our deck (painting by Brooks Wilson, 2011)

Our Terrigal holidays were a wonderful time of family togetherness. In the day times we would surf or walk down the beach to the lagoon, where we could rent canoes or paddle boats. Sometimes we would walk to Bob's Beach at the far end of the main beach. This was quite a long walk and when Andrew was around five, he would get tired along the way and would end up having to be carried. When we got there, we could snorkel and watch the fish.

Sailing was also an activity we enjoyed. Our catamaran sail boat was on a trailer and we would launch it at the boat ramp in Terrigal harbour. Once we got past the breakwater into the ocean, it could get quite rough and the sail boat could tip over, which it often did. It was a major effort to right the boat and get back on board.

The Hobbie Cat sail boat from wall hanging in Terrigal

When the children were out by themselves this was of great concern to us as parents. We would stand on the beach and watch them. We had a back-up plan, involving another boat owner, if they got into trouble. Fortunately, I think we only used this once.

In the evenings we would get together with John and Judy Goddard and their children, Simon, and Jeremy. Often the men would cook, and we'd have BBQs. After dinner we would play charades.

Now, in 2021, we still have the beach house which we have now owned for forty years. Our children have grown up, married and we have grandchildren. During the summer, each family spends some time there. I often go too, and particularly enjoy walking down the beach at sunrise and having coffee at the surf club. Our dog, Jefferson, used to come with me.

My friend 'Jefferson'; Warrawee (2011 circa)

Over the years Terrigal has changed. It previously was like a small country town. It now has a major hotel, up-market restaurants, and high-rise apartments.

Overseas trips were also part of our family experience. We had "home leave" back to the US every two years. When we made these trips, we also went to other countries as well: Europe in 1975, Africa in 1977 and South America in 1979.

On our European trip in 1975, Cynthia's daughter, Lisa, came with us and continued on to Sydney. She stayed in Australia for nine months, both living with us as well as getting experience working on a farm. She had just completed High School and had taken a year off before going to college. We got to know Lisa well, and we still feel remarkably close to her. She now lives near Portland, Oregon, with her husband Brock. They have two adult children, Hunter, and Katie.

Cynthia's son, Greg, also came to Australia a few years later, after he finished High School. We loved having him. He lived with us briefly before getting a job on a farm three or four hours away. He purchased a motor bike so he could ride back and forth.

On one occasion I remember Greg arriving back in Sydney after his long motor bike ride. We immediately played tennis on a court we owned down the street. Greg won.

As the years went by our children married and our family grew with the arrival of spouses and grandchildren. Our Family Tree is shown in Appendix 1.

Having an extended family was something Ann and I were delighted to have. We took this larger group on several overseas trips to give everyone an interesting experience and in the hope our grandchildren would bond and form life-long friendships.

The first overseas trip as an extended family was to Ohio in 2008 when we sold the farm; the second was to South Africa in 2012 to visit Game Parks; the third was to Uluru (Ayers Rock) in Central Australia in 2015.

The family on safari; South Africa (2012)

The last overseas trip was to Lake Tahoe in California, in July 2018. Nineteen members of our family came. Ann's niece, Lisa Metcalf, made all the arrangements. We stayed in beautiful cabins on the Lake's edge right next to where Lisa and Brock had their house and were staying. Lisa, and Brock's son, Hunter, was there too.

Lisa's brothers, Greg and Andrew Scott, came as well. Greg came with his friend, Julie Briggs, while Andrew came with his wife, Lisa, and their children Talia, Baden, and Landen. Talia developed a close friendship with John Wilson's daughter, Emma, and with Andrew Wilson's daughter, Lucy. The girls are still in regular contact by email and phone and Talia is now talking about having her Gap Year in Sydney after she finishes High School.

4th July weekend with family; Lake Tahoe, CA (2018)

In the last two years of Ann's life, she developed Fibrosis of the Lung which made it harder and harder for her to breath. She never complained but during this period she was on oxygen support and wheelchair bound. Throughout this period Ann was greatly helped by our long-term friend and Pastor, Paul O'Sullivan.

She passed away on April 2, 2020.

In looking back, I feel how lucky I was to have had Ann as my wife. We had the same values and the same interests. We put our family first.

It is now May 2022. All our grandchildren are progressing with their lives. In Andrew and Fran's family, Hugo has completed three years of Law and has gained Distinctions in most subjects. He has one more year to go. Anna has completed one year of Nursing and loves her course. Charley and Lucy have three more years of school. Charley is at Knox where he does well at school and loves basketball. Lucy is at Abbotsleigh. She also loves school and is the captain of her Soft Ball team.

In Mary and Graeme's family, Caleb has one more year at the International Sports School on the Central Coast where he is a keen tennis player. His long-term aim is to do social work and help people with their lives. Eli is at a special school for disabled people. Eliza is also at the International Sports school and is a star soccer player. She has been selected to play for a Central Coast Mariners team which gives her special training. Her aim is to eventually play for Australia.

In John and Sue's family, Emma has three more years to go at Roseville College, an Anglican Girls School. At the end of 2021 she gained Academic Honours for the third year in a row. She plays soccer and basketball, and enjoys playing the guitar. Louisa has one more year at Greenwich Public School prior to going to Roseville College. At the end of 2021, she was made Vice Captain of her school for 2022.

I am immensely proud of our grandchildren and what they are achieving. I know Ann would be too.

In the remaining time that I have, my central aim is to continue the work that Ann and I were doing together. That is to keep helping our children and grandchildren in whatever way I can.

Additional photos for Chapter 5:

Ann at her family's home; Springfield OH (1955)

Five Ways Church; Killara NSW (2021)

CHAPTER 6

Our Home in the US

Elcamere Farms was our home in the US whenever we visited. It was close to Springfield where Ann had grown up and it was a place we loved. It had been in Ann's family since 1806 when ancestors on her mother's side had taken up land in the newly formed state of Ohio.

The farm, itself, consisted of 1,300 acres of very rich agricultural land. It was flat country with deep soil and regular rainfall. It produced corn, soy beans and pigs.

Painting of Elcamere Farms by Brooks Wilson

The name, Elcamere, was derived from the names of family members: "El" for Ellie, Ann's mother, "CA" for Cynthia and Ann, and "mere" for the family name Meredith.

We visited the farm at least every two years and often more frequently after I joined Pittsburgh based Koppers Company in 1965. Most of the visits were during the US summer of July and August.

The only place to stay on the farm, initially, was in the cabin, a secluded place near the main house where the farm manager, Charles Penrose, lived with his wife Rebecca.

The cabin was one room with bunk beds, a small kitchen and flush toilet and electric power. Outside there was a BBQ. attractive trees and a small pond nearby with ducks swimming. We would often sit on the front porch and admire the scenery.

We enjoyed staying there.

Cabin behind the main house, with Charles and Rebecca Penrose; Elcamere Farms (1987 circa)

Ann and Cynthia inherited the farm when their mother passed away in 1975. At that time Cynthia and her husband Mike took responsibility for the farm, as they lived in Washington DC and we were too far away living in Sydney.

Cynthia subsequently wanted to sell her share so we bought her out in 2002.

This date more or less coincided with my retirement, which meant we had more time to travel. We took over the farm house on Stewart Road, and made it our own.

Stewart Road House; Elcamere Farms

We visited Lowe's Store and bought furniture. We had a carpenter fix up the kitchen. Our bedroom was on the second floor. I remember there were 18 steps in the stairs leading up to it. We put a BBQ on the outside deck so on long summer evenings we could cook and eat dinner overlooking the farm. We had beautiful views of pastures in the foreground with a dense forest behind. At times we could even see deer. Cynthia often drove down from Cleveland and stayed with us. We also joined the Springfield Country Club where we ate frequently, played golf occasionally and swam in the pool. Jim Baker, who had grown up with Ann, would often join us for dinner.

Farm land from back deck of Stewart Road house

From time to time we also went to the Springfield Methodist church which had been part of Ann's life and also to the church near the farm in Plattsburg which had been built by Ann's ancestors.

All these activities allowed us to connect with Ann's early life and people she had known. This included having three girls who had grown up with Ann fly in from various parts of the country and spend a weekend with us on two occasions. Our children, also, joined us from time to time.

On one of our trips Ann and I found where the original farm house had been located. It was quite a distance from our Stewart Road house and was on land no longer part of the farm near Beaver Creek. We found the foundations of what had been the house and we also found a cemetery nearby where family members had been buried. The marble engraved stones had all fallen over and were covered with weeds.

Charles and Rebecca Penrose were the key to making the farm work. Charles had run the farm for over 50 years having been appointed by Ann's dad. He was very hard working and loyal. In later years he was assisted by his son, Michael.

One of my great pleasures was to work with Charles doing whatever had to be done. I had farm boots and clothing I kept at the farm. In a way it reminded me of my early life when I had worker at Mount Desmond. Charles knew everything about the farm - when to plant corn and soy beans and when to sell. He also knew all about the pigs that were bred on the farm. He could fix all the farm machinery. On top of this he had a very nice manner.

Elcamere Farms, OH: Charles and Rebecca Penrose

Before we sold the farm in 2008, we took our entire family of 19 people to a farewell function at the farm. Cynthia and her three children and their families came too. The photos on the next page show some of the people who were there. We were particularly pleased that cousins from the US and Australia were able to meet.

This was a large gathering. Some people stayed in the Stewart Road house. Others stayed in two caravans we had rented. We had a farewell catered dinner in a large marquee next to the house.

Charles Penrose and his family were at the dinner. Special mention was made of the key role Charles had played.

Farewell lunch with extended families; Elcamere Farms, OH (2008)

We were sad to sell the farm. It had been a key part of Ann's life forever and a key part of my life since we were married.

Additional photos for Chapter 6:

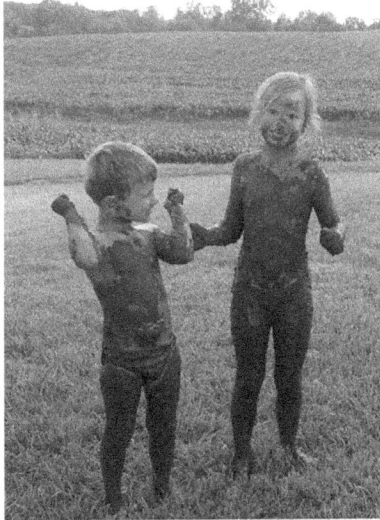

Caleb and Anna playing in the mud; Elcamere Farms (2008)

Photo taken during visit to Elcamere with the Scotts and Bama; Elcamere Farms, OH (1975)

Painting of Steward Road house (Painting by Brooks Wilson, 2007)

Caravans assembled in field for accommodation

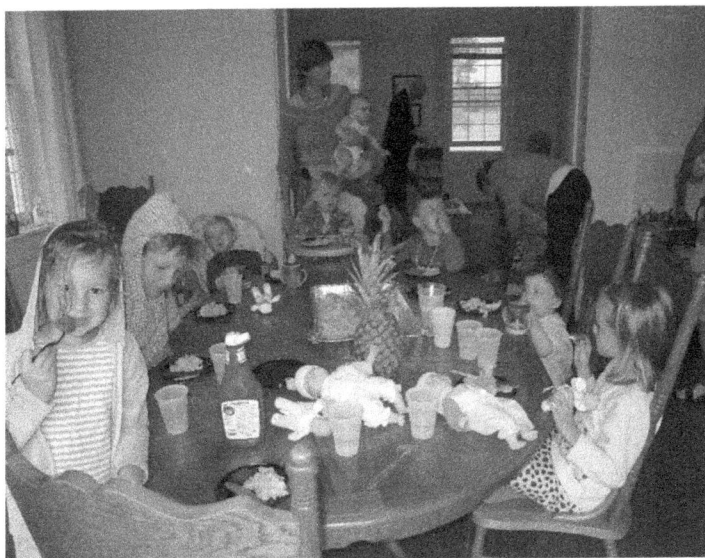

Dinner with kids in Steward Road house

Brooks talks with Charles Penrose on tractor; Elcamere Farms

CHAPTER 7

Helping Family in Times of Need

14 April 2013 to 16 January 2014

This chapter explains the role Ann and I were able to play in the lives of Mary's children after they had been put into foster care. They were ultimately allowed to live with us for nine months before returning to their home.

It is a story of the love we had for Mary, and her children and the role we were able to play in showing this love.

Because what happened was such a major event in all our lives, I am telling this story in some detail.

Our farewell dinner; Warrawee NSW (16 January 2014)

It was early December 2012 when Mary invited me to spend the forth-coming weekend of December 8-9 at our Beach House with her family. Ann was in hospital and this was Mary's way of reaching out to her dad. Mary sounded in great spirits and I accepted her invitation with pleasure.

At this time Caleb was eight, Eli was six and Eliza was four.

Then at 3pm on Wednesday, December 5, just a few days before the week-end, I received a distressed call from Mary. The Department of Community Services (DOCS) had picked up Caleb and Eli from their schools and were holding them in Protective Custody at their Chatswood office. They had also asked Mary and Graeme to deliver Eliza to their office as well.

The next step was to be a meeting at their office at 6pm that evening. It was agreed I could come too.

What a surprise! I had never dreamed that this could happen with our family. Ann and I were very close to Mary and her children, visiting them at least weekly and having them sleep over at our place where they each had a bed. I had a particularly close relationship with Caleb as from age five I had taken him to breakfast most Saturdays at the Restaurant - Echo on the Marina - near the Roseville Bridge. After our breakfasts we had gone down to the water and skimmed rocks.

We knew that Mary had had mental problems but she had had treatment and seemed to be better.

I went to the meeting on December 5 and arrived at 6pm shortly before Mary and Graeme. This gave me a chance to talk with the DOCS worker who received me. He said DOCS had taken the children into custody as Mary and Graeme had shown themselves incapable of looking after them. He said the children were currently in a back room in their office and would shortly be taken to foster homes.

I responded that if DOCS felt they had to take the children away to pro-tect them, then the best place to send them would be to us, their maternal grandparents. The children knew us well and they all had beds at our place where they slept often.

The DOCS worker said the children could not go to us now as we had not been "assessed" and this process would take around three weeks. He indicated that if I tried to push him too hard now, he would call the police.

Mary and Graeme arrived at the meeting. Further discussion along the same lives continued, and the meeting broke up. We did not see the children.

I left the meeting feeling great distress. I knew the children would be feeling completely lost. They had been taken away from their home, family and total sense of security.

Caleb told us later that he thought he had been put into kid's jail for something he had said or done. The only way he had been able to survive was to sit in a corner of his room and cry.

The problem became even more stressful for him when he later asked a DOCS worker when he could go home. He was told when he was eighteen in ten years' time!

Over the next few weeks Ann and I were assessed. Two young women from DOCS came to our home and over a two-hour period questioned Ann and myself separately. They wanted to know about our own individual upbringings and what kind of parents we had been to our own children.

One question they asked was had we ever smacked any of our children. I said, yes, but only once or twice.

There was also a concern about our age as we were both eighty.

The DOCS assessment report was issued on 9 January 2013. It stated that Ann and I were not suitable carers for a number of reasons which included our age and the fact we had once used physical punishment on our own children.

To counter this finding, we immediately started legal proceedings to have the DOCS determination overturned.

This was a long-drawn-out process; we had no idea when it might end or what the end result would be. All we knew was that as long as the children were living in external foster homes, we and their parents were only allowed to have short visits with them every few weeks.

The first such visit was at the DOCS office in Liverpool on December 20, 2012 at 2pm for one hour. The children had been driven there separately; Caleb from one location and Eli and Eliza from another.

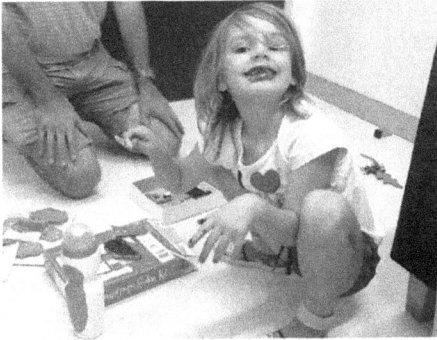

Graeme and Mary with daughter, Eliza; Liverpool NSW (December 20 2012)

The room where we met was small and jail-like. There was a DOCS person present who recorded everything that was said.

We had taken Christmas presents for the children. Most of our conversation was about this.

As the meeting broke up, I told Caleb I was looking forward to having breakfast with him at our usual restaurant as soon as the children came back to us. He asked if I had been to the restaurant since he left. I told him I would not be going back there until he was with me.

The children then got into their cars and were driven off.

What kind of a meeting had this been? It made us feel we were living in a Police State where the individual had no rights and the children no longer belonged to us.

Other meetings followed in 2013; Fairfield on 11 and 28 January, Liverpool on 16 February.

Fairfield, NSW (January & February 2013)

At Bigge Park in Liverpool on 16 February we had a soccer ball and were able to kick this around with Caleb. When it came time to leave, Ann's comment was that Caleb seemed like an old man who was being dragged away.

At this meeting, and at later ones, we were able to get some information from the children about their lives and how they were being treated.

What we found out was this:

- Caleb was living with a family in Newtown.
- Eli and Eliza were living with a family in Campbelltown.
- Over the Christmas period Eliza and Eli had been driven to Adelaide and back by their carer who was visiting people there. The carer's boyfriend had gone too. (*What kind of child protection was this? It seemed like a very irresponsible act on the part of DOCS to allow this*).

- For the first six weeks of the new school year Eliza did not go to school.
- During this same period Eli went to school for only two hours per day.
- The children had no phone contact with their parents or anyone they knew.
- They all wanted to know when they could come home.

All the above showed us the children were completely cut off from people who loved them and from everything they had known. This made us redouble our efforts to have them live with us.

We hired a respected Child Psychiatrist, who was known to the Court, to assess the suitability of Ann and myself being made carers. He interviewed the two of us and the three children on 8 April 2013. This was the earliest date he had available. He spoke to each of us in turn and saw how we all interrelated. He subsequently wrote a report dated 23 May 2013. which indicated we would be suitable carers.

Just three days after we had seen this Psychiatrist, a Court Hearing was held on Thursday, 11 April 2013.

At this hearing the key document to be considered was an Affidavit dated 4 April 2013 written by the Case Worker responsible for the Familton children. Copies of this Affidavit had been sent to the Court, the Psychiatrist plus Ann and myself.

Because the Affidavit stated Ann and I were not suitable Carers, we wrote a Rebuttal on 6 April 2013 and sent this to the Psychiatrist. Our Rebuttal outlined how the children would benefit through living together with us, as opposed to separately as at present, and being with grandparents who loved them. We also stated that in living with us the children would be returning to their previous schools and old friends. We stated we had the funds to get any help we needed. This included having a live-in Au Pair and a cook to prepare evening meals.

The Caseworker was then cross-examined by our Barrister on the substance of her Affidavit. He asked her how long had she been on this case? The answer was "three weeks". He then asked her had she ever seen Ann and myself together with the three children? The answer was "no". Then at 11.45am the Psychiatrist was contacted by phone and interviewed over the loud speaker. He said he had met with Ann and myself and our three grandchildren on 8 April and gave a brief summary of his findings. He said he had read the case worker's Affidavit and that he had also received a Rebuttal from Ann and myself. He agreed to email a copy of our Rebuttal to the Court.

At this point the Hearing was adjourned for lunch with the Caseworker lined up to cross examine me when the Court resumed after lunch.

This cross examination never occurred. During the lunch break DOCS agreed to settle the matter and allow the children to go into our care.

This decision was implemented promptly. The children were delivered to our home on Monday, 14 April.

What excitement this was for Ann and myself. It was one of the happiest days of our lives. Our family had been re-united!

Eli, Eliza and Caleb eating ice cream and reading a story; Warrawee NSW (14 April 2013)

The nine-month period in which the children lived with us worked perfectly. We quickly settled into a routine. Ann and/or I would drive the children to school and also collect them. As we drove along, we would play "I spy with my little eye...". Back at home we would play soccer on the lawn and Ann would help Caleb with homework. Dinner was always at 6pm. The Au Pair organized baths. At bed time we would tuck them in, hear their prayers and have a brief talk. Caleb frequently asked when he would be able to go back to his parents.

The people who helped us during this time did a great job. This included the young women Au Pairs who came from Germany, France and Thailand. They each stayed with us for three months. We also had a great cook, Deb Bartlett, who came often. She became a close friend and is someone we still see.

Our friend, Pastor Paul O'Sullivan, also played a key role in helping Caleb.

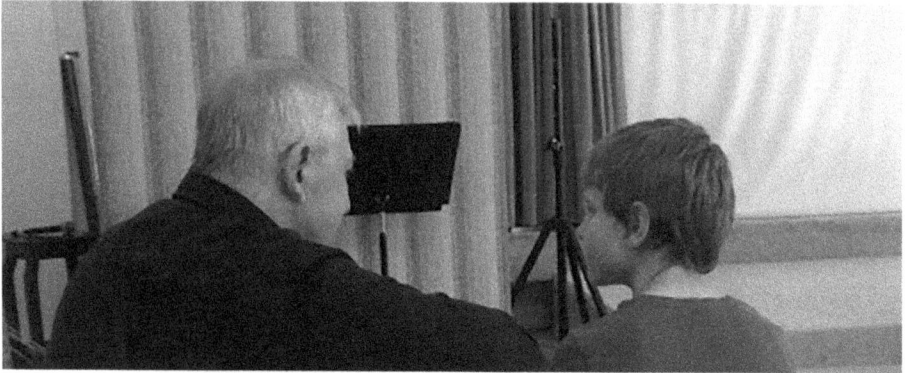

Paster Paul O'Sullivan checks in with Caleb; Mona Vale, NSW (2013)

Throughout this time, we were also very much involved with school activities. This included going to school concerts and sporting events.

I particularly remember the first time I took Caleb back to his old school in Frenchs Forest. He had friends who came up and give him a hug. They were delighted to see him back.

We got to know the teachers well and also our grandchildren.

As time went on there were further Court Hearings on the question of when the children could return to their parents. The Psychiatrist wrote another Report after interviewing Ann and myself, the children and their parents. His conclusion was that the it was safe for the children to return to their parents with DOCS and the grandparents having an oversight role.

So, on 16 January 2014 we had a farewell dinner at our home. A photo was taken of the children and grandparents. A copy of this photo is still on our refrigerator.

The children returned home next day.

During the time the children were living with us, Caleb and Ann had many conversations about religion. Ann had a great religious faith as did Mary and Graeme. Caleb developed this too.

Caleb had one last conversation with Ann on 1 April 2020. the day before she passed away. Ann was lying in bed in Palliative Care. Caleb stood at the end of the bed and told her what he was doing and showed her a video he had prepared about his aim in life. Ann encouraged him in what he was doing and told him she loved him.

The Memorial service we had for Ann some ten months later was attended by over one hundred people. Our children, Charles, John, Mary and Andrew all spoke lovingly about their mother. Charles was the M.C. Some of the grandchildren also spoke including Andrew and Fran's daughter, Anna (18), who read a poem, John and Sue's daughters Emma (14) and Louisa (10) who played Minuet and Mary and Graeme's son Caleb (16) who spoke and played a special music piece on the piano he had written in memory of his grandmother. The response from the audience was loud applause.

Now, in the second half of 2021 Mary, Graeme and their family have been back together for seven years. They now live on Brisbane Water in the Central Coast where they have a motor boat and enjoy life together. The children are happy at their schools. Caleb and Elisa go to the International Sports School in the Central Coast where Caleb plays tennis and Elisa plays soccer. Eli goes to the Glenvale School where he gets special help. They all attend the Connect Church in Umina.

The fact that Mary's family is now reunited is one of the great joys of our life.

CHAPTER 8

Searching for the Right Job

Brooks aged 21 (1954 circa)

After graduating from Harvard Business School, I knew my aim in life was to run a company. I also knew I had to gain prior experience if I were to achieve this.

What was the best first step to take?

In May 1957, at the end of the academic year at Harvard Business School, there were lots of job interviews including one with the American Smelting and Refining Company (Asarco) which had a controlling interest in Mount

Isa Mines in Australia. They were looking for people to work with them in New York for eighteen months, prior to going to Mount Isa.

I accepted this job as I felt working in New York would be good experience and the job in Mount Isa, working for the Chairman, sounded interesting.

My job in New York was at Asarco's head office, 120 Broadway, close to Wall Street. I worked in the Accounting Department as an assistant to the Chief Financial Analyst, Charles Link, with whom I shared an office. Charlie gave me various financial studies and guided me through them. He was a good teacher and a good friend. He ultimately became Godfather to our oldest son, Charles.

As I have written in Chapter 5, I met my future wife, Ann, in New York City. We were married on 18 April 1959 and arrived in Mount Isa in July 1959, ready for me to start work.

The Chairman of Mount Isa Mines was a great boss and I very much enjoyed working for him. The first assignment he gave me was to write a speech he that he was to give about the mining industry in Australia and how the major mines were discovered.

By way of getting background material, he had me meet with historian Geoffrey Blainey who had recently written a book on the history of Mount Isa Mines. I met Geoff at his home in Melbourne.

The speech was written and given, and other similar assignment followed. At the end of eighteen months, I realized I was not a mining engineer, and I would have to find another job if I wanted to achieve an executive position.

We left Mount Isa in January 1961 and moved to Sydney to join the management consulting firm; W.D. Scott Pty Ltd. Walter Scott was a leading Australian businessman. In the four years I spent with the company the job I liked best was opening new markets for Australian businessmen in Asia. This was the time when the UK was joining the Common Market in Europe. As a result, Australian firms would no longer have preferential treatment in selling to the UK. This meant they had to look for other markets which is where I came in. I made many trips to Japan which was then the emerging market for Australia.

But still the thought in the back of my mind was how do I get a job that would eventually allow me to run a company? To join an existing Australian company might be a hard slog to get to the top. By contrast, if I could find a new US company wanting to set up in Australia, this might be the way to go.

What did I have to offer? I thought it was this:

- My education in both Australia and the US.
- My American background which included my work experience plus family relationships.
- My Australian background which included my experience in Asia as well as having a father who was successful in business and well known.

So, I placed an advertisement in the "Wall Street Journal" stating what I have just described. A week later, by pure coincidence, my mother invited Ann and myself to come to lunch to meet some friends who were visiting from the US - Ken and Alice Sandbach. My mother had known Alice from Paris Hill.

We went to the lunch. Ken explained that he worked for a Pittsburgh based company, Koppers, and that he was in Australia to talk with BHP about the possibility of setting up a joint venture.

I said nothing to Ken at the time about my job interest. But a few days later when he had returned to the US, I sent him a copy of my "Wall Street Journal" advertisement. He immediately wrote back "Don't make a move before talking with me."

So, to cut a long story short, I did join Koppers in April 1965 and worked in a two-man office with Ken in Sydney. The joint venture with BHP was formed in March 1967 and in March 1970 I was appointed Managing Director. This became my job for the rest of my business career.

As I look back, I was very lucky to find this job. I knew what I wanted, but how could I find it? I learnt from this experience that there is a lot of luck in life, and that when an opportunity appears It must be grabbed, or it is lost forever.

A quotation from Shakespeare's Play, Julius Caesar, speaks to this point.

> *There is a tide in the affairs of men*
> *When, taken at the flood, leads on to fortune.*
> *Omitted, all the voyage of their life*
> *Is bound in shallows and in miseries*
> *On such a full sea are we now afloat*
> *And we must take the current when it serves,*
> *Or lose our ventures.*

Chapter 9 talks about my career with Koppers.

Reflections On My Time with Koppers in Australia, the US and China

My business career from age 32 to 65 was with Koppers USA, a company I joined in May 1965, in Sydney.

During this period, while I lived and worked in Australia, I had a very close association with the US and with China as I will outline.

Koppers, with Head Office in Pittsburgh PA, was one of the top one hundred companies in the US. It was an industrial products company building steel plants and operating coal tar distillation plants processing a by-product from steel making. It was also in the timber treating business and owned gravel quarries.

The first Koppers person to visit Australia was Ken Sandbach, Vice President Far East Operations, who came in 1965. His mission was to have talks with BHP top management about the possibility of forming a joint venture to process BHP's by-product coal tar.

The idea of having such talks came from two people who met at Harvard Business School. They were Gordon Darling, then a Director of BHP, and Bill Jackson, who then headed up the Coal Tar Division of Koppers.

Gordon and Bill recognized the possibility of synergy between their two companies. BHP produced steel which meant they had coke ovens that produced coke, a product used in the steel making process. A by-product of producing coke was coal tar. Koppers was the largest coal tar distiller in the

US turning coal tar into naphthalene, coal tar pitch and creosote, all saleable products used in the production of further industrial products.

At the meeting in Melbourne attended by Ken, it was agreed that Koppers should undertake a feasibility study to see if setting up a new coal tar distillation business in Australia was viable.

BHP offered to give any help required.

To get things moving Ken set up a two-man office in Sydney. I joined him.

My job, initially, was to work with Bob Garvin who came from Koppers Head Office to conduct a market survey in Australia. Where was the market for coal tar products and how large was it?

I liked working with Bob. He was very professional in what he did; people were pleased to give him information. He found there was a growing market for coal tar products, particularly coal tar pitch used by Aluminium Smelters in making carbon anodes, a key ingredient in their process.

A special memory I have of Bob is the time he came to our home in Gordon for dinner. He came early and took our sons Charles (aged 5) and John (aged 3) for a ride in a billycart. What a nice thing to do.

The next person to visit was Ed Losch, who came to determine the cost of building a coal tar distillation plant in Australia and where it should be located. The key question - was the investment viable?

His study showed that it was, and a copy of this Report was provided to BHP.

So early in 1966 a meeting was held in Melbourne with Sir Ian McLennan, then BHP's Chief General Manager. I was part of the Koppers delegation. At this meeting Sir Ian said that he accepted Ed Losch's report and agreed that a joint venture between Koppers and BHP should go ahead.

As we left the meeting I said to Sir Ian, "My father asked me to pass on his best wishes". Sir Ian searched through the name cards and saw my last name was Wilson. He said, "Is your father Bob Wilson from Grazcos?" I said "Yes". My father's reputation had helped me form an on-going connection with Sir Ian.

By way of example, in 1976 I was highly active in the Australian American Association. Because it was the Bicentennial of the founding of the United States, we had organized special functions in Sydney which included US Vice President Nelson Rockefeller as guest-of-honour at a dinner. I invited Sir Ian to this dinner, and he came.

As I look back, it was the work that Ed Losch did that was the key to getting Koppers established in Australia. He was a Chemical Engineer who had joined Koppers on graduation from the University of Pennsylvania. He had taken leave of absence to serve in the US Navy for three years during the Korean War. Ed and his wife, Shirley, became close personal friends and we kept in touch right up to the time that Ed died in November 2019.

After the meeting in Melbourne, I had an interesting experience back in Sydney. It was early December and tennis matches were being played at White City in Sydney as a prelude to the Australian Open. One afternoon, Ken said "Let's take the afternoon off and go to the tennis." When we arrived at the Stadium Ken asked an attendant if he could meet the manager of the US team. This man came to the gate. Ken introduced himself and the response was, "Ken Sandbach, the football star?" Ken replied that he was. We were then invited in to sit in the grandstand with the US team. I sat next to Arthur Ashe who was a world-famous player.

Until that time Ken had not spoken about his football prowess. It turns out that when he was at Princeton University, he was a star quarter-back football player and won the "All American" award. People who followed sport knew his name.

Ken Sandbach in press photo for University Tigers; Princeton, NJ (1934)

With BHP and Koppers having agreed to set up a new business in Australia, Koppers Australia Pty Ltd was registered as a 50/50 joint venture between Koppers and BHP. We called the new company KAP to distinguish it from the US parent. The new KAP coal tar plant was located in Newcastle and was officially opened in May 1967 by Sir Robert Askin, Premier of NSW.

Koppers Aust Pty Ltd's (KAP) Coal Tar Distillation plant; Newcastle, NSW

At this stage, Ken Sandbach, and his wife Alice, returned to the US. They had become close friends of our entire family. When Ken retired some years later, they came back to Sydney where they lived until they both passed away.

With KAP now established, Koppers appointed a management team. John Fencil, who had run the Koppers sales office in New York City headed the team. Tom June, an experienced Plant Manager, was to run the operation in Newcastle, and Mike Tallarico was appointed Plant Engineer. I was chosen as Marketing Manager to work with John Fencil in Sydney.

The team worked well together, ably supported by John Crawford, and John Lowcock in Newcastle who had operated the previous BHP Coal Tar Plant.

While Koppers appointed the management team, it was BHP's job to appoint the Chairman. The first Chairman appointed was Jack Richards, a former Rhodes Scholar. Jack had worked at the steelworks in Newcastle as a young man and was close to Sir Ian.

Jack not only ran our Board Meetings but also produced innovative ideas to help the company. When a major steel natural gas pipeline was to be installed from Central Australia to the East Coast, Jack recognized that the pipes had to be protected against corrosion. Coal Tar Enamel, a product manufactured by Koppers, had been specified.

Jack said, "We've got to get into this", and KAP won the tender. We made and supplied all the Coal Tar Enamel required on this pipeline and others.

The next part of the story is tragic. At the time that Jack was Chairman of KAP, he was also involved with the Esso-BHP gas field in off-shore Victoria which was then under construction. He and a colleague had driven there one night to check up on progress. On the way back to Melbourne they had a fatal accident and Jack was killed. John Fencil and I went to his funeral.

On the KAP business front, John Fencil taught me a lot. He had superior product knowledge and related well with customers. I took over from him when he returned to the US in 1970.

From this point the company grew quite quickly due to the increasing number of aluminium smelters being built in Australia and other countries.

We ultimately supplied coal tar pitch to the five smelters in Australia, plus smelters in New Zealand, Western Canada, Bahrain, Dubai, and Iran.

Koppers Aust Pty Ltd's (KAP) ship, SeaKAP Coal Tar Pitch tanker

Opening these markets involved a lot of travel. We were an Australian producer and a world supplier.

Ships supplied most of the smelters, with loads of up to 6,000mt at a time. We eventually purchased our own ship to manage this business.

As a result of our growing market, we needed more feedstock than BHP could provide. So, we went to Taiwan and purchased all the coal tar from their steel plant, China Steel, on a long-term basis.

When we eventually needed even more feedstock, we wondered if China might have surplus coal tar, or coal tar pitch that they could sell to us. So, we went there to find out.

As I explain, below, we were successful in finding new opportunities in China. Because this experience was my most interesting time with KAP, I will tell the story in some detail, including the Historic Tour of China given to us by the Chinese government after we opened our plant in Anshan.

On our first trip to China, in May 1980, our party consisted of John Lowcock, our Chief Engineer in Newcastle, Colin Newell, Chief Financial Officer and me.

At the time of our visit, we didn't know much about China. I had read "Red Star Over China" by Edgar Snow that spoke about the Communist Revolution and the Long March. I also knew that Mao's Cultural Revolution (1966-1976) had caused economic havoc as educated leaders were sent to the country-side to work with peasants. Deng Xiaoping had reversed this policy and opened China to the outside world in 1978. In a famous statement he had said he didn't care if a cat were black or white, as long as it could catch mice. This was his way of breaking from the hard-liner Communist approach that everything was about equality. The real challenge, he said, was to increase the standard of living of the people. He further believed that the Chinese people would accept the leadership of the Communist Party if it achieved this.

With the help of the Australian Trade Commissioner in Beijing we met with the China Metallurgical Import Export Corporation (CMIEC). The person we met there was Vice President Fei Zuxun, who became a long-term friend. (Sadly, he passed away on 8 August 2021). We told him we were looking for a source of coal tar or coal tar pitch to bring to Australia. He suggested we should visit several steel plants and have discussions with them.

Before we went on these visits, we could see in Beijing that China at that time was not an advanced country. Everyone rode bicycles and there were very few cars. We also recognized that the Chinese people had not seen many foreigners.

This came home to me when I rented a bicycle and joined the throng. I managed to get lost and stopped to ask a young man on the road-side directions to the Beijing Hotel. I knew enough words in Chinese to be able to ask this question.

The young man answered in Chinese. I, of course, could not understand and shrugged my shoulders. He thought I must have been deaf, so he shouted in my ear. I shrugged again; we both laughed.

I eventually got back to the hotel.

Over the next two weeks we visited a number of steel plants and had found nothing. Fortunately, our luck changed just before our last day in China when we were back in the CMIEC office in Beijing. There we met Mr. Zhao Gui Chen from the General Chemical Works of the Anshan Iron and Steel Company, then China's largest steel plant.

Mr. Zhao thought there could be an opportunity for us at his plant. He suggested we delay our return home and come to Anshan.

Anshan is in Liaoning Province in Northeast China. This Province had been part of Manchuria, the area forcefully taken over by the Japanese in 1931. The Japanese had built the steel plant we were visiting. There was a rail line linking Anshan to the Port of Dalian.

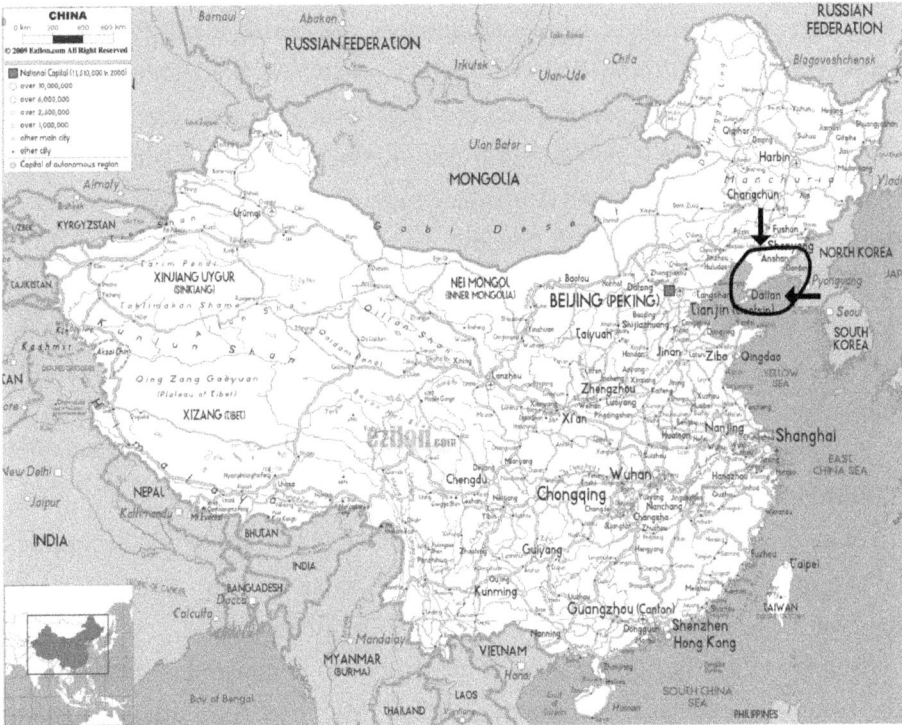

Map of China, showing Dalian and Anshan

The Russians had upgraded the tar plant at Anshan during the time when China looked to them for modern technology. Unfortunately, we found this plant was not able to manufacture the product we needed.

After we returned to Australia, we sent our engineers to Anshan to design the type of tar plant we would need. Collaborating with Chinese engineers they determined what it would cost to build this plant and the rail cars to carry our solid pencil pitch to Dalian where we planned to build a storage shed and a loading system, from the shed onto ships.

During this period Mr. Zhao, and a team from China, also came to Newcastle to see what we had accomplished there. Mr. Zhao became a long-term friend, and we are still in touch with him.

The result was the construction of a new coal tar distillation plant in Anshan, along with rail cars and the building of a large pitch storage shed in Dalian. Australian and Chinese engineers worked together to make this happen. We agreed to pay half the capital cost and Anshan agreed to sell us specified quantities of coal tar pitch over a 10-year period at a reduced price.

Called a Compensation Trade Agreement, this was the first venture of any type to be agreed between an Australian and a Chinese company and worked for the mutual benefit of both parties.

Through working with Chinese engineers, we got to understand how their system worked. We built a personal relationship between our two groups, and we became friends. We went on bushwalks together through the very scenic countryside around Anshan.

Friendship also extended into the political realm.

When I was in Dalian, I called on the mayor. It was mid-summer and hot. I had been told that the mayor had saved someone in the surf, so I congratulated him on this. He said, "Would you like to go for a swim?" I said "Yes". So, the two of us headed off to the beach and went swimming.

By mid-1983 the construction of all plants was completed. We held opening ceremonies in both Anshan and Dalian. My wife, Ann, attended, along with John Lowcock who had managed the project from our side, Peter Laver from BHP who was also Chairman of KAP, and the Australian Ambassador, Hugh Dunn.

Completion ceremony for the JV's new Coal Tar Pitch plant; Anshan China (1983)

After the ceremonies Mr. Fei took Ann and me on a two-week Historic Tour of China, courtesy of the Chinese Government. There were just the two of us plus Mr. Fei and an interpreter. We visited five separate locations and learnt about Chinese history going back 4,000 years. We not only visited historical sites; we learnt about Tang Dynasty Poetry and the Analects of Confucius.

One of our favourite pieces from Confucius was the following:

> *The Master said: "At fifteen I set my heart on*
> *learning; at thirty I took my stand; at*
> *forty I came to be free from doubts; at fifty*
> *I understood the Decree of Heaven; at sixty*
> *my ear was attuned; at seventy I followed*
> *my heart's desire without overstepping the line.*

We enjoyed all the places we visited, and Ann wrote a full report of what we did.

Some highlights:

Big Wild Goose Pagoda (with Mr Fei); Xian, China (1983)

- In Xian we had an unusual experience as well as seeing the entombed warriors. We were told the story about Concubine Yang and Emperor Xuanzong of Tang who was very much in love with her. We were shown a building with a secluded court yard where Concubine Yang used to have a bath. Ann and I were invited to have a bath in the same place. We did. It was a nice sunny day, and the water was warm. Our friends waited outside.
- In Nanjing we saw the two-mile-long bridge, finished in 1968, linking both banks of the Yangtze River. This was the first time North and South China had been joined together in this manner.
- In Hangzhou we visited the "Six Harmonies Pagoda" named for the six codes of Buddhism. We liked this code as it seemed to us to have universal application to marriages everywhere.

The six codes of Buddhism:

> *living together*
> *no argument*
> *same hobby*
> *same beliefs*
> *same point of view*
> *same profit*

- In Shanghai we stayed in a magnificent guest house, surrounded by acres of gardens, where Chairman Mao Zedong used to stay. Ann wrote "We ate the most delicious variety of foods I have ever tasted. My favourite dish was fish cooked in vinegar sauce."
- Canton (Ganzhou) was the last place we visited. Ann wrote that, after eating yet another delicious spread of dishes, and spending the night at the new modern Dong Pang Hotel, we boarded a ferry and headed down the Pearl River to Hong Kong and home.

Nanjing: Tea Gardens

Bikes outside village

Xian: two soldiers resting

Xian: two children outside the
Big Wild Goose Pagoda

1983 China visit with Ann and Mr Fei

As I write this chapter, it is now 2021 or 38 years since we were on this Historic Tour of China. I am so glad Ann was with me. We had a wonderful time and a unique experience.

As I look back, I also think about what the Chinese people have been through over the centuries and in more recent times. I think about the Japanese invasion of the 1930s, the Civil War which ended in 1949, and the Cultural Revolution of 1966-76. It is only since then that poverty has been largely eliminated.

Because we had a 10-year deal with China I went back there at least once a year to check up on how things were going. At the end of one of my trips my Chinese friends asked if there was anything else I would like to see in China.

Because of the importance of "Confucian Thought" in China I said I would like to see where Confucius was born. So, a trip was organized for me. It involved a night trip in a ship from Dalian across the Gulf of Bohai. I was given the captain's cabin. Then when we arrived at the Port of Qingdao in Shandong Province there was a two-hour car ride to Qufu where Confucius had lived. Along the way the car got bogged and we had to push it.

In 1986 I was Chairman of the Australia-China Business Council (ACBC). We had our Annual Conference in Beijing. Leading Australian and Chinese businessmen were there with speeches made by Australian Prime Minister Bob Hawke and Chinese Premier Zhao Ziyang.

I met the Chinese leader at the meeting. As he was leaving, he looked up at me and said in a very friendly way (through an interpreter). "Do you play basketball?" I said "No, but I'm thinking of taking it up."

We both laughed. I liked Zhao for his willingness to reach out as he did.

At that time Zhao was a key man in China. He had played a significant role in fostering economic growth in his country through allowing a degree of private ownership.

My interest in China extended to our daughter, Mary. In 1988, at the age of twenty-three, she went to Beijing to study Mandarin. She was there for 15 months and became fluent in the language.

In 1989 the Tiananmen Square student insurrection came along. Zhao Ziyang, (now General Secretary of the Party) had argued for a peaceful resolution and went amongst the students massed in the Square urging them to stop their seven-day hunger strike and go home. He promised consultations with student leaders would then go ahead.

While some students were sympathetic to what Zhao was saying, many were not, so the sit-in continued. Hardliners in the Chinese leadership believed the only way to end the insurrection was by force. The Army was sent in, and many students were killed.

Australian Prime Minister Hawke wept when he heard this news. He allowed all Chinese students currently in Australia to remain if they wished.

Zhao Ziyang, who had argued for a peaceful resolution, was banished from the Party, and put under house arrest for the rest of his life.

A week or so after the Tiananmen incident, Ann and I were invited to a dinner at the home of the Chinese Consul General in Sydney. Fellow guests were NSW Premier Neville Wran and his wife, Jill, and the respected heart surgeon, Dr. Victor Chang.

The aim of the dinner was to assure us that the massacre in Tiananmen Square had been forced on the Government and that they still wanted our support in moving ahead. I could understand their point of view.

In the early 1990s I met Hawke again at a dinner hosted by the Governor General in Canberra in honour of a visiting Chinese leader. I asked Hawke about Zhao. He said he was still in touch with him.

One final comment about China: In December 1999, the Australia China Council (an arm of the Australian Government) gave out awards to "individuals from Australia and China who have made outstanding contributions or achievements in areas of Australia-China relations". I was presented with the Business Award for my "key role in the signing of the first Australian joint business venture with China in 1981". Ann came with me to the Award Ceremony held in Adelaide where I was given a gold-plated medallion that I still have. (Appendix 4)

I accepted the award on behalf of all my colleagues in Australia and China, who had worked tirelessly to bring this project to fruition.

Apart from our success in China, we had other areas of growth within KAP. We acquired two companies that became Divisions of KAP. The first was the timber treating company, Hickson, that had treating plants around Australia. The second was Continental Carbon which operated a Carbon Black plant in Sydney.

One of KAP's Timber Treating Plants

These companies had their own management structures which basically continued with the same autonomy they had had previously. An additional benefit these companies gave to us, apart from an enlarged business, was an increased management pool. In fact, the former Managing Director of Continental Carbon, Mark McCormack, ultimately became Managing Director of KAP.

Over the years people in Koppers USA played a key role in what we did in Australia. One was the chairman of the company, Fletcher Byrom.

Fletch was one of the most interesting people I have ever met. He had wide interests and was a great chairman of Koppers. His aim was to get his management team totally involved. He did this by delegating and having them responsible for results. His view was that people learn by their mistakes.

In doing this he was not a "soft touch". People were allowed to learn by their mistakes as long as they didn't make them too often.

He was also a great public speaker with an international reputation. The Australian Institute of Directors, for instance, was one group that had him speak at their annual conference in Sydney.

On this visit and others, Fletch made contact with BHP's top management in Melbourne. He knew the key people as friends.

Dick Spatz was another Koppers executive who made a significant contribution to KAP. Dick ran the Forest Products group within Koppers and had a close relationship with the Hickson Corporation in the UK. Hickson's had a timber treating business in Australia which ultimately became part of KAP.

An unexpected opportunity for KAP occurred in 1988 when Koppers USA was acquired in a hostile takeover by the Beazer Corporation of the United Kingdom. The Beazer company wanted the gravel quarries owned by Koppers and not the Coal Tar or Forest Products Divisions.

Bob Wagner, who then ran the Forest Products Division, put together a management buyout of the Coal Tar and Forest Products groups. Bob's lawyer friend, Clayton Sweeney, assisted him in this buyout. The newly formed company was called Koppers Industry Inc., in which the Beazer Corporation owned 40%, KAP 40% and a management group 20%.

I joined the Board of the new company and over a 10-year period attended Board meetings in the US three or four times a year until I retired.

Shortly before I retired, BHP sold its shares in KAP to Koppers Industries.

Koppers Industries still exists and is listed on the New York Stock Exchange. It is a global company with current annual sales of $US1.7 billion.

A final comment on my role within KAP: As Managing Director of KAP, I was responsible for profitability and growth. To achieve this, I made the acquaintance of the Chief Executives of all our major customers, and I delegated as much as I could within KAP so that other executives had a sense of ownership.

I also attempted to reach out to our workforce as I recognized that everyone had a key role to play, whatever their job, in making the company successful.

As an example of how I did this. On one of my visits to our timber treating plant in Western Australia, I arranged a dinner for the entire workforce of around thirty people.

At the dinner we had round tables with six people to a table. I had it arranged so the management group was spread around and not sitting together.

At my table I had fork lift drivers and people who ran the treating plant. I went around the table asking each person to speak in turn about their family and any outside interests they had. I shared my story too.

What I found out was amazing. The fork lift driver and his wife gave money each year to an Aboriginal group in Western Australia. To help raise money for this, his wife drove a local bus. Then another person at the table said that each year he and his wife went to South Africa during their annual vacation to help a Christian group with construction in a small village.

I was very touched by what I learned at my table. I felt I had also achieved my goal of making people at the table realize that whatever their job, we were all part of the same team.

In looking back at my career with KAP, whatever we achieved, the credit goes to my very capable colleagues who gave their best. It was a privilege for me to have been their leader.

Over the period 1970 - 1998 we were able to increase earnings at a compound rate of 20% per year.

A magazine writeup about KAP is included in Appendix 2.

I retired from Koppers at age 65 in 1998 after a remarkably interesting career.

CHAPTER 10

My Other Activities

During my business career, and after, I was involved in a number of outside interests covering the following categories:

1. Australian – American Relations
2. Knox Grammar School
3. Business Associations
4. Government Boards and Study Groups
5. Business groups
6. Charities

1. Australian -American Relations

Australian-American Relations were important to me because of my background. Early in my career I was involved with the following groups:

Harvard Club of Australia

HARVARD CLUB OF AUSTRALIA

Harvard Club of Australia crest

When Ann and I settled in Sydney in 1961 we were keen to make friends. Meeting other people who had been to Harvard seemed like a good thing to do so I set about forming the Harvard Club of Australia.

The Harvard Alumni office sent me the names of all Harvard Graduates living in Australia plus a Constitution we might want to adopt.

I was one of the first Harvard Master of Business Administration graduates living in Australia, but there were other people who had studied Law, Architecture, Education, Dentistry, and other subjects at Harvard. I contacted one person from each Faculty area and asked them to join me in forming a local Harvard Club. They all agreed.

I then approached Professor Julius Stone who was one of the best-known graduates on the list and asked him if he would be willing to be President of the Club. He agreed.

Having this part organized I then approached Prime Minister Menzies asking if he would be the Australian Patron of the Club. He agreed. He had previously been awarded an Honorary Degree by Harvard.

Harvard Club Australia, Harold Holt and Prime Minister Robert Menzies

I also approached the US Ambassador in Australia, Bill Battle, asking if he would be the US Patron. He agreed. This was of no real surprise as he had been appointed by President Kennedy who had a strong Harvard connection.

The next step was to set up a date and place for an Inaugural Meeting, which was done.

The inaugural meeting of the Club was held on November 21, 1961, at the Hotel Australia. The Club was formed, with Julius Stone elected as the first President. I was Secretary.

Jim Wolfensohn returned to Sydney in early 1962 and we co-opted him onto the committee. Jim went on to play a key role in the Club's activities. He instituted the Menzies Scholarship scheme to raise money to send Australian students to Harvard. A special dinner was held to launch the scheme attend by the leading citizens of Sydney. Prime Minister Menzies was Guest-of-Honour and Guest Speaker. He said how honoured he was to have his name linked to such a scheme.

Enough money was raised at this dinner to award the first Harvard Scholarship.

Jim left Sydney shortly after this dinner to work in the United Kingdom, initially, and then in the United States. He had a spectacular career in finance serving for 10 years as President of the World Bank. Jim never forgot his Australian origins and over the years was the largest contributor to the Menzies Scholarship scheme.

Now, in 2021, ninety Australians have been awarded Menzies Scholarships to Harvard.

The Harvard Club of Australia continues to play a key role in fostering exchanges between Australia and Harvard which have been very much to Australia's benefit.

Australian American Association

Australian American Association crest

The Australian American Association was set up in Sydney during World War II when one million American soldiers passed through Australia on their way to the islands to our north. The Association was still highly active in the early 1960s when I first became involved.

Leading Americans spoke at our functions, including Richard Nixon in the early 1960s shortly after he was defeated in the Presidential election by Jack Kennedy. George H.W. Bush also came when he was Vice President.

I served in key positions in the Association, including in the role of President.

My main contribution in fostering Australian-American relations was by organizing an Australian-American Festival in Sydney in March 1976, to coincide with celebrations in America to mark the Bicentennial of the US. Over 150 Australian organizations participated with the "Sydney Morning Herald" publishing the daily program of events. The US government strongly supported what we were doing and arranged for leading American citizens to participate. This included Vice President Nelson Rockefeller, Nancy Kissinger, author James Michener and John Warner who had been Secretary of the Navy and who later became a US Senator from Virginia.

Nancy Kissinger had been in the same year as Ann at Mount Holyoke College and came to our home for a BBQ along with her Secret Service detail.

Fostering good Australian-American relations was important during this time as the Whitlam Government had been in office until late 1975, with some Government Members being anti-American.

Because of the role I played in organizing the Australian American Festival and getting leading Americans to visit Australia, I was awarded the Australian decoration - Member of the Order of Australia (AM). Appendix 3.

2. Knox Grammar School

Dr. Ian Paterson was the headmaster of Knox while our sons were there, starting in 1970. He was a great Headmaster, full of ideas and a tireless worker. The school, under his leadership, achieved academic success and school numbers grew. He introduced new initiatives including violin playing for every boy and annual productions of school musicals that involved Abbotsleigh girls as well. He set up Camp Knox on the Hawkesbury River which had Outward Bound activities. He was always at school sporting events on Saturdays and was the last to leave. He knew most boys by name, particularly those in their final years.

When Andrew, aged thirteen, had to go to Houston for an operation, both Ian and Marjorie Paterson came to our home. This shows the personal concern they had for their students. And when Andrew was in the Texas Heart Institute, he received a bunch of flowers from Knox tied with blue and black ribbons which were the Knox colours.

Andrew recovered and went back to school. Ann and I then continued our involvement with the school as Knox parents.

Ann served food at the Tuck Shop. She also worked closely with Christina Dennis in organizing Knox Garden Days held in early Spring.

In my case, the Knox Foundation had been set up in 1977 to raise money for the construction of new School Buildings and to create a Trust Fund that could subsidize school fees or award scholarships in the future. The headmaster, Ian Paterson, had introduced this initiative. I was invited to be Chairman of the Foundation and I accepted.

For the next few years, I worked closely with Dr. Paterson at fund raising events. The headmaster would outline the vision; it was my job to ask for financial support. The Knox community supported what we were doing. Money was raised to finance the construction of the music centre and the gymnasium.

The Trust Fund was also well supported and by 1990 it had reached $18 million.

When I retired as Chairman of the Foundation, I was presented with a painting of the school with particular focus on the new music centre.

Painting presented to Brooks in recognition of his role as Chairman of Knox Foundation showing the Music Centre and the Gymnasium constructed during his tenure

In 1979 I was invited to join the Knox Council. I served as a Council member until 1999, the last three years as Chairman. During my period as Chairman, Dr. Paterson retired, and Peter Crawley was appointed as his successor. Peter Crawley was a pioneer in the use of computers in education and he had them installed at Knox with every student having a lap-top.

Now more time has gone by, and more Wilsons have gone to Knox. They are Andrew's sons (and my grandsons). Hugo graduated in 2018 and Charlie will graduate in 2024. In that year Knox will be one hundred years old and the Wilsons will have been part of Knox for 82 years.

In looking back over my long involvement with Knox I can say it has been a rich experience. I have come to recognize the great contribution made by Knox (and schools like it) to our community. The key ingredients of what makes it work so well, I believe, are as follows:

- Knox passes down values from one generation to the next. The values are the principles on which the school was founded - honesty, fair play, do your best, learn how to lead, and to observe Christian values.

- Parents send their sons to Knox as they appreciate these values, and they know their sons will get a good education which includes high academic achievement and the all-round development of the boy. They also appreciate the teaching of self-discipline which comes through having school rules that are enforced.

- Teachers obviously have a leading role both in imparting knowledge and as role models. Therefore, Knox needs to continue to hire the best and find ways of keeping them challenged and motivated.

- Training in leadership is an important ingredient of what Knox offers, as the principles learnt at school - through doing - will guide students for the rest of their lives.

- In all this the headmaster has the key role as it is he who brings all aspects of the school together. He is the internal and external spokesman for the school. His vision, drive and personality will permeate throughout the whole school.

- The School Council also has a key role. The first requirement is to appoint the best person available as Headmaster and then to work with him.

Knox Grammar School Newsletter

3. Business Associations

Because of the international nature of our business at KAP, over the years I participated in a variety of Business Associations related to our field of expertise. I served a period as chairman of Councils concerned with China, Taiwan and Fiji.

The list includes:

- American Chamber of Commerce

- Australia-China Business Council
- Australia-Korea Business Council
- Australia-Taiwan Business Council
- Australia-Fiji Business Council
- Pacific Basin Economic Community
- Committee for Economic Development of Australia

4. Government Boards and Study Groups

For the State Government of NSW, I was on three government owned business boards:

- Pacific Power – (Electricity generation)
- Pacific Solar (Solar panel research)
- State Transit Authority (Busses and Ferrys)

For the Federal Government I was involved in:

- Export Finance Insurance Corporation.
- The Group studying the best way to introduce MBA programs into Australian Universities.
- The Tertiary Education Commission that allocated Government funds to universities and other Tertiary Education providers, based on their needs.

5. Business Groups

After I retired from Koppers, I served a period of time on the board of Atlas Copco Australia. In addition, I also maintained my association with two former colleagues in the United States. The people concerned were my friends who had also retired.

Dick Spatz

The first person was Dick Spatz. Dick had served in the US Army during World War II and had been in the Battle of the Bulge. After the war he had trained as a lawyer and at Koppers, when I met him, he headed up the Forest Products Division.

Through this job he was close to Hicksons in the United Kingdom, who were in a similar business in their own country as well as in Australia. When I was running Koppers Australia, Dick and I went to Castleford in the UK and persuade Hickson to sell their Australian business to us.

As a result of making this trip Dick and I got to know each other well.

When Dick retired from Koppers he started a business of his own, which was de-acidifying books held by the Library of Congress. Many of the books in their collection were printed on acidic paper and as a result were slowly disintegrating. Under Dick's system, the books to be treated were packed up at the Library of Congress, sent to Dick's plant in Pittsburgh and then sent back to Washington. Many books were treated this way.

Dick asked me to help him open overseas markets. I was pleased to do this. I went first to Japan to investigate the possibility of treating books held in their government collections. I remember being shown State Papers in Tokyo. There was a full-time guard on duty and in the long corridors where the collection was held there were signs of damage caused by World War II.

Nothing eventuated from this visit. The people concerned did not want to send books or documents out of their own country. The same answer applied to Libraries both in the UK and Australia which I investigated.

The company still exists today and has operations around the world, particularly large deacidification plants in the US and Japan treating both bound volumes and loose manuscripts, as well as sales offices in Canada, Spain, and the Netherlands. There are also partnerships in Poland and Russia. (For further information, see: https://ptlp.com).

Fletcher Byrom

My next experience was collaborating with the Retired Chairman of Koppers, Fletcher Byrom.

Fletch was someone I admired tremendously. He had been a great leader at Koppers. He delegated down and got the best out of people. He was prepared to let people make mistakes as he believed this was how we all learn. He also thought about the issues of our day and had well thought out views on these.

Fletch had come to Australia several times when I was running KAP. On these occasions I had gone with him to visit the CEO of BHP, Sir Ian McLennan, both at BHP and at his home, and to look at the Iron Ore mines in the Pilbara.

Fletch had also given a major speech at the Australian Institute of Directors Annual Meetings in Sydney. This was well received. As a result of all of this I got to know Fletch well.

So, some years after we had both retired, on one of our trips to the US, Fletch invited Ann and me to spend a few days with him and his wife, Peg, at their home in Carefree, Arizona. We were pleased to accept.

During our visit Fletch told me he was a metallurgist by training and that he was working with a group on developing a new process for making tungsten carbide. He asked me to join with him. He would pay any transportation costs and there would be a success fee if the project went ahead. I agreed to join with him.

Fletch had a new way of making tungsten carbide which involved heating ground tungsten in a furnace and injecting carbon dioxide gas during the process. A company in Pittsburgh called Pittsburgh Mineral & Environmental Technology, Inc. (PMET) did the lab work, and it was my job to buy the tungsten in China.

The company I visited in China was Xiamen Tungsten in Fujian Province, which is the source of a significant supply of the world's tungsten. My friend, Mr Fei, came with me.

We purchased the tungsten, and PMET turned it into micro particles of tungsten carbide which a Pittsburgh company, Oberg Manufacturing, tested in their process. Unfortunately, the tungsten carbide produced this way did not work out.

6. Charities

Over the years I worked for a range of charities that included the following:

- North Shore Heart Research Foundation
- Lifestart – working with children with a disability
- Outward Bound
- Opportunity International Australia (OIA)- working in the area of world poverty relief.

The North Shore Heart Research Foundation is doing significant research. I was pleased to join the board and help raise funds as one of the founders was Dr. Gaston Bauer who had looked after our son Andrew.

Lifestart was another organization I was pleased to help as our grandson, Eli, has Down Syndrome. I served on the Board and was involved in the selection of Sue Becker, the current chief executive, who has done an outstanding job.

Outward Bound was an interesting organization with a global reach. I served as Chairman in Australia and was on the International Board. Ann and I both met Prince Philip. I went to meetings in Windsor Castle, Bermuda, and New York. I also took part in a three-day walk in Scotland.

Opportunity International Australia (OIA) is the group in which I spent the most time. Over the years I served as Chairman of OIA and was also on the International Board in the US and on the Board of a Micro Finance Bank in the Philippines. Our mission was to lend small sums of money to poor people (mainly women) to enable them to start a business.

By way of example, In the Philippines many unemployed people had come to Manilla looking for work and not finding any, lived under bridges. A small loan enabled a woman to start a hairdressing or other similar business. In total we had a million clients in the Philippines.

We also operated in many other countries as well. Ann and I visited clients in Russia, China, Zimbabwe, and South Africa.

Helping people get out of poverty is still one of the major world-wide issues of our time. It transcends international rivalry between counties.

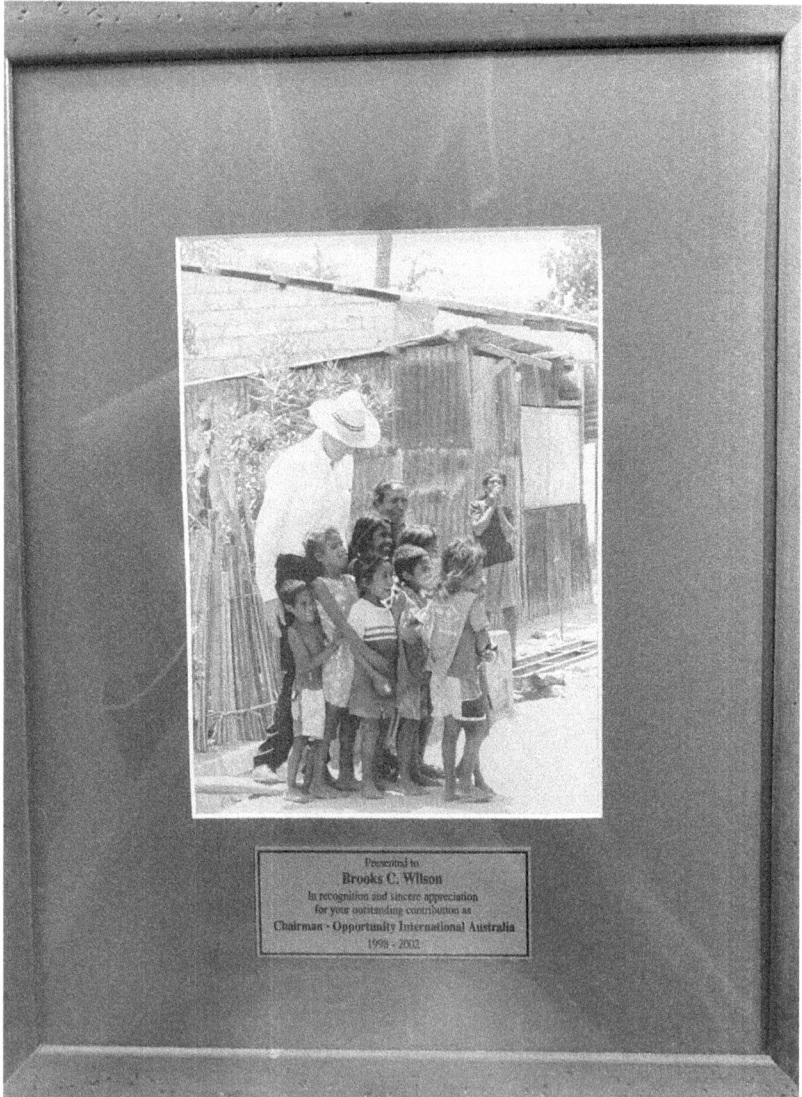

Presented to
Brooks C. Wilson
In recognition and sincere appreciation
for your outstanding contribution as
Chairman - Opportunity International Australia
1998 - 2002

Photo presented to Brooks upon his retirement from the board of OIA

CHAPTER 11

Remembering Previous Generations

The interesting thing about life is that we all go through the same life cycle whenever we live. The differences between the generations are caused by the times in which we live. Each generation must face the challenges of their times.

With this in mind, I decided to research the lives of two of my great grandfathers - one on my father's side and one on my mother's side. What challenges did they face and how did life turn out for them?

And I wondered, did any of the attitudes or characteristics I saw in my great grandfathers come down to me?

The reason I picked these two ancestors was that I had detailed information on each. For my Australian great grandfather, John Henry Wilson, I had seen where he lived and grew up in Ireland and I had also seen where he lived in Tasmania. In addition, my father had often spoken about him, and I had a source of family history written by my cousin Michael Wilson.

In relation to my American great grandfather, William Eustis Brooks, I found a book published after his death giving details of his life. His son, Clayton, my grandfather, gave me a Bible which had special writing in the front. This will be explained.

The story which follows outlines who the great grandfathers were and how they coped with major challenges at an early age that changed their lives.

Henry John Wilson (1827 - 1904) – Australia

Tasmania: Henry John Wilson

Henry John Wilson, my father's grandfather, was born in 1827. His father was Benjamin Wilson and his mother was Sarah Frances Partridge. He was born in the family home, "Sledagh Hall", on their plantation a few miles from the port city of Wexford, Ireland. Henry was the youngest of eight siblings; he had five sisters and two brothers.

At the time of his birth and until his late teens, his family was well off. Their plantation was part of the feudal system under which the Wilsons were Lord of the Manor and Irish peasants rented land from them and grew potatoes. This "rent" was the Wilson's source of income.

The Wilsons had owned the plantation since 1670. The British had become Protestant in 1534 under Henry VIII while Ireland remained Catholic. The British wished to subdue the "unruly" Irish, so they expelled Irish landlords and inserted British ones who had to employ a certain number of Protestant people and build a Protestant church. This is what my ancestors did.

Ann, and I plus our son Andrew, visited Wexford in 1989 and went to Sledagh Hall and the church built by the Wilsons found in a nearby small town called Mulrankin. It was obviously a family church as on the wall was a large plaque commemorating Colonel Nicholas Wilson who had been killed at Cawnpore during the Indian Mutiny on 28 November 1857. In the church yard we also found the graves on Henry John's parents, Benjamin, and Sarah Wilson.

County Wexford, Ireland: Sledagh Hall

Henry received his early education at the Diocesan School at Wexford and then on 1 July 1845, aged 18, he entered Trinity College, Dublin, to study Theology. As the third son it was his role to enter the church; his oldest brother was to inherit the property and his middle brother was to join the army. This was the custom at the time.

Henry's uncle, Colonel Nicholas Wilson, (whose memorial plaque was on the wall in the church), made an interesting comment about his nephew at this time. He said it was a pity to put a strapping young fellow like Henry into the church; he should be in the army. He offered to ask his friend Lord Wellington to give Henry a commission should he wish to pursue this option. Henry did not take up his uncle's offer.

In the year Henry entered Trinity College a blight destroyed the potato crop in Ireland. As a result, tenant farmers received no income and landlords received no rent. Most people thought this was a one-off occurrence and that things would get better, but they didn't. The blight lasted four years, and at the end of this time the Wilsons could no longer afford to keep Henry at Trinity. He had to leave before he graduated.

What should he do next?

His older brother, Edward, (known as Ned), had gone to Canada and was an Officer in the Royal Canadian Rifles. Henry decided to go to Canada too and try farming. It was 1849 and he was 22.

On arriving in Canada Henry lived with his brother in the barracks, before moving to a farm in Lower Canada.

Farming in Canada did not work out. After two years he was not making any money, he didn't like the freezing winters and he was lonely. He wanted to try something else. But where would that be?

His mother knew of his predicament and contacted her sister, Charlotte, in Tasmania, to see if Henry could go there. Charlotte and her husband, Jocelyn Thomas, lived on their farm, North Down, near Port Sorell.

Family values were important to the two sisters; the response from Charlotte was immediate; they would welcome having Henry come to Tasmania.

Henry accepted the invitation. He borrowed funds from his parents, (which they ultimately gave him), and on 18 January 1852, at the age of 24, sailed from New York to Melbourne on the sailing ship *Baltimore*. There were 260 passengers on board. They arrived in Melbourne on 28 May 1852 after a voyage of 133 days.

As soon as they got off the ship, Henry and a ship-board friend named Willis, went to the goldfields in Ballarat, hoping to get rich before going to Tasmania. They were somewhat successful in finding gold, but after nine months decided it was time to leave. They walked to Melbourne, taking their gold to the bank, and receiving one hundred sovereigns in exchange. The only gold Henry kept was a small piece that he subsequently made into a tie pin.

The tie pin became an heirloom within the family, and it was passed down through the generations. Henry gave it to his son, Chris (my grandfather) who in turn gave it to his son (my father) Rob. My dad gave it to me and I in turn gave it to my son Andrew who was the only member of my family at that time who had a son. Unfortunately, the story of the tie pin ends there. Someone broke into Andrew's house and stole all his wife's jewellery, including the tie pin.

After a short stay in Melbourne Henry and Willis took a steamer across Bass Strait to the Port of George Town in Tasmania. Then after a two-day trek they reached the Thomas family property, North Down.

Henry was pleased with what he saw. The farm was situated on the coast with splendid views of the ocean. It was 1,660 acres, had good soil and was very productive. More importantly, his aunt made him feel welcome and he had cousins there his own age.

North Down, Tasmania: view of farmland and coast

As Harold Thomas wrote in his book, "The Story of North Down", Sam Thomas, Henry's cousin, who was running the property at that time, set Henry and his friend Willis up growing potatoes. They received a good yield and decent prices the first year, but poor results in the second year. As a result, Willis decided to give up farming and go back to the goldfields.

Henry decided to stay in Tasmania.

A surviving photo shows Henry to have been a handsome man with a good build. He obviously spoke with an Irish accent as his friends in Tasmania called him Paddy.

In 2004 my cousin, Michael Wilson, organized a re-enactment of Henry's trip from the time he landed in Tasmania to his arrival at North Down. Michael trekked part of the way himself and had a row boat take him to the edge of the farm at Port Sorell. Snow Thomas, son of Harold, who was running the farm at that time, was waiting on the beach to meet him.

Family members came to Tasmania for the re-enactment. This included our children Mary and Andrew and their families. We hired a room at a nearby hotel called Hawley House. Snow Thomas and Michael spoke about their experiences. I mentioned that we had a silver cup in our home that had been given to Henry Wilson by the parishioners of the church he attended. Andrew's son Hugo, aged 4, said he had seen that cup.

Tasmania became the place where Henry spent the rest of his life. He married his cousin Louisa Sophia Thomas in March 1857, when he was 30.

A year after his marriage, Henry received a letter from his father, Benjamin. The one page of the letter which remains communicates the love the father had for his son, and it also tells us a lot about Benjamin.

Sledagh
March 1ˢᵗ, 1858

My dear Henry

Your letter to your dear Mother giving an account of yourself and wife, made me in my old days, so truly thankful to Almighty God for his undoubted goodness and care of you in this uncertain and precarious world after all your trials and changes that you had to contend with, and may the Almighty in his great Mercy shower blessings on you and yours. Ever will be your old father's prayer for your wife from whom every blessing in this fleeting life comes and let us all miss the chastening rod and say with David, it's good for us to have been afflicted. I congratulate you in the account of your stock crops, etc. and your owing no money, but good will to everybody.

Your mother told me your good intention of paying back the money got for you on going out.

We insist on your never to think about it, as it is only the few pounds of interest that we pay and the money will be your own when it pleases God to remove us from here, and may God prepare us all for that awful moment. You will have heard before this reaches you of your poor Uncle Nicholas being knocked down at the head of his Regiment - a great loss for his young family. Your cousin, Fred, has got his Ensigncy in his poor father's Regiment. They will be well provided for. I had a letter from your uncle a short time before your aunt went last out of his leaving in the English Funds, something about twelve thousand pounds chiefly saved since he went to India: his pay as Brigadier General for the last seven years being so good which cost him, poor fellow, his life. He died nobly as a soldier, and as a true Christian in the atonement of his merciful saviour, once (inside) for us all miserable sinners. Dear Ned (Henry's brother) left us about six weeks back to join his Regiment (in Canada). You will be rejoiced to learn that he has got his Company and has by the augmentation to his Regiment got five Captains under him so that he can no longer call himself the old Lieutenant. His promotion afforded us all such heartfelt...and your good mother not least as you well know...

The letter ends at this point.

After they were married Henry and Louisa lived with Louisa's mother, Charlotte, (then a widow) for 25 years in the original house called "Old North Down", before moving to a small farm Henry had purchased adjacent to North Down called "Larooma" where they had cows and made cheese. They had four sons, the second of whom was my grandfather. Henry never returned to Ireland and while he did not become an ordained minister which was his early intention, he did become a lay reader in his church.

When he retired from his position as Lay Reader, he was presented with a silver cup which has been passed down through the generations, and I now have.

Cup presented to Henry John Wilson from parishoners

Etched on the cup are these words:

H. J. Wilson
From the Parish of
North Down
1891

1897 circa, Tasmania: Henry John Wilson holding his grandson,
Robert Christian Wilson (Brooks' father)

Henry died in 1904 at the age of seventy-seven.

Did Henry have a happy life? On the positive side he had a family of his own and also a farm. On the negative side he missed the life he had known in Ireland. In Tasmania he was only a small-scale farmer, not the "Lord of the Manor" his family had been in Ireland. There were also times when he felt lonely. In a letter to his son, Chris, (my grandfather) on August 25, 1897, he wrote "I feel miserable sometimes as I have no friends in Tasmania, and I pine for those that are gone".

While there were negatives about his being in Tasmania, I think, on balance, Henry had a better life in Tasmania than he could have had in Ireland or Canada. In Tasmania he had close relatives who were also farmers as he was.

In looking at his life overall, I wondered if any of his values and ambitions were passed on to succeeding generations, including my own? It may have been the desire to succeed in order to live the type of life he had known in Ireland. His son Chris, my grandfather, may have inherited this aim. He left Tasmania at the age of 18 to go to the mainland of Australia to build up a land holding of his own. He ultimately created a large farm of 7,000 acres in Mudgee, NSW. In doing this he overextended himself financially and after twenty years had to sell what he had and buy a smaller property in Blayney.

Chris's son, Rob, my father, was in the Light Horse in Palestine during World War I. He tried farming after the war but after a brief period gave this up and became the chief executive of a successful sheep shearing and wool blending business (Grazcos). This was at a time when wool was Australia's main industry. He was also on major company boards and a community leader ultimately becoming Sir Robert Wilson. I, too, as a young man had a great desire to succeed and became the Managing Director of a company at the age of thirty-seven. All this "desire to succeed" may have come from talk of Sledagh Hall and what the family had in Ireland. I was told about this family background at quite an early age.

William Eustis Brooks (1835 - 1906) - USA

William Eustis Brooks

William Brooks was my mother's grandfather. He was born in Kingfield, Maine on June 6, 1835. He was the son of George and Anna (Eustis) Brooks.

The story of William's life was printed after his death and contains what was said about his life at his funeral. This is a most interesting account and the fact that it was published shows the esteem in which he was held. A copy of this book is kept in the Brooks family house in Paris Hill, Maine.

In looking at William's life overall, I am impressed with how he coped with the difficulties of life and still achieved his goals. He never gave up.

At the age of ten he had the devastating experience of being orphaned with the loss of both parents. No child could have a greater loss. Fortunately, his grandfather, William Eustis, a Church Deacon, became his foster father giving him both love and spiritual guidance.

As a result of this experience William developed a belief in God and Christianity which became the central feature of his life. He also knew from a young age he wanted to become a church minister.

After he graduated from high school, the way ahead for him was to go to college first, and then on to Graduate School to gain a theological degree. But his family had no money to pay for this. How could he get the money? The only way he could see was to join the California gold rush.

California Gold diggings

In February 1855, at the age of 19, William and three close friends went from Maine to California to look for gold. There was no overland route, so they sailed from New York on the steamer "North Star" down the east coast to the isthmus, crossed to the west coast by horse and carriage, then sailed up the west coast to San Francisco and the goldfields. Quite an undertaking. They stayed there two years. When it came time to come home William made a reservation on the steamer "Central America" to travel back down the west coast. He had a last-minute change of plan and couldn't join the ship. This was fortunate as this ship sank with total loss of life. On a subsequent ship William got home safely.

William made enough money on the goldfields that he was able to enter Waterville College (now Colby College). He graduated with a bachelor's degree, with honors, in the Class of 1862. He was 27.

Shortly after he graduated William married Angie Richardson Wilson, the daughter of Rev. Adam Wilson D.D. on August 8, 1862. They picked this date as ten days later William was to become a soldier in the Civil War. They both wanted to be married before he went.

On August 16, 1862, William was mustered in as a first lieutenant in Company E, 16th Maine Regiment Volunteers. He was in the campaigns of Maryland, including South Mountain, Antietam, and other battles under McClellan; then in the battle of Fredericksburg under General Burnside in which he was wounded on December 13, 1862. He continued in service under General Hooker until honourably discharged as captain of his company on a surgeon's certificate.

16th Regiment Maine Volunteers, Battle of Antietam

In 1865 William entered Yale Theological Seminary, New Haven, Connecticut and graduated in 1867. Having this degree allowed him to be a Congregational Church Minister which became his vocation for the rest of his life. He received an Honorary Doctor of Divinity Degree from Colby College in 1890.

William and Angie had five children the youngest being Clayton K. Brooks, my grandfather, who was born in 1874.

In looking at William's life overall, did he have a happy life? It seems to me he did. He had achieved his goal of being a respected theologian and he had a family of his own. His contemporaries saw him as a man of his word.

How did William's life affect later generations? All I know is that his youngest son, Clayton, my grandfather, gave me a Bible when he and my grandmother, Grace, visited us in Australia in 1938. I was five years old. The Bible had a beautiful red cover with my name embossed in gold on the front and I still have and treasure it.

Inside this Bible my grandfather had written these words:

Brooksey
Let the Word of God be the Rule and Guide of your Life.

*May it bring you Comfort in times of Sorrow; Strength in times of
Weakness;*
Courage to always do the Right in times of Prosperity.
With love
Your Yankee Granddad
Clayton Kingman Brooks
1938

The truths of what he wrote had perhaps come from his father and have
now come down through the generations to me.

CHAPTER 12

Poems that I like

There are many poems that I like. I have included two, below, that relate to life itself and how to live it.

Mortality

By William Knox 1789-1825

Oh, why should the spirit of mortal be proud?
Like a swift-fleeing meteor, a fast-flying cloud,
A flash of the Lightning, a break of the wave,
Man passes from life to his rest in the grave.

The leaves of the oak and the willow shall fade,
Be scattered around and together be laid;
And the young and the old, and the low and the high,
Shall molder to dust and together shall lie.

The infant, a mother attended and loved,
The mother, that infant's affection who proved,
The husband, that mother and infant who blessed,
Each, all, are away to their dwellings of rest.

The maid, on whose cheek, on whose brow, in whose eye,
Shone beauty and pleasure—her triumphs are by;

And the memories of those who have loved her and praised
Are alike from the minds of the living erased.

The hand of the king that the sceptre hath borne,
The brow of the priest that the mitre hath worn,
The eye of the sage, and the heart of the brave,
Are hidden and lost in the depth of the grave.

The peasant, whose lot was to sow and to reap,
The herdsman, who climbed with his goats up the steep,
The beggar, who wandered in search of his bread,
Have faded away like the grass that we tread.

The saint, who enjoyed the communion of Heaven,
The sinner, who dared to remain unforgiven,
The wise and the foolish, the guilty and just,
Have quietly mingled their bones in the dust.

So, the multitude goes, like the flower or the weed,
That withers away to let others succeed;
So the multitude comes, even those we behold,
To repeat every tale that has often been told.

For we are the same that our fathers have been;
We see the same sights that our fathers have seen;
We drink the same stream, and we view the same sun,
And run the same course that our fathers have fun.

The thoughts we are thinking, our fathers would think;
From the death that we shrink from, our fathers would shrink;
To the life that we cling to, they also would cling;
But it speeds for us all, like a bird on the wing.

They loved, but the story we cannot unfold;
They scorned, but the heart of the haughty is cold:

They grieved, but no wail from their slumbers will come;
They joyed, but the tongue of their gladness is dumb.

They died--ah! they died--and we things that are now,
Who walk on the turl that lies over their brow,
Who make in their dwelling a transient abode,
Meet the things that they met on their pilgrimage-road.

Yea! hope and despondency, pleasure and pain,
We mingle together in sunshine and rain;
And the smiles and the tears, the song and the dirge,
Still follow each other like surge upon surge.

'Tis the wink of an eye, 'tis the draught of a breach,
From the blossom of health to the paleness of death,
From the gilded saloon to the bier and the shroud:
Oh, why should the spirit of mortal be proud?

(This was also Abraham Lincoln's favorite poem)

It's All in the State of Mind

by Walter D. Wintle

If you think you are beaten, you are,
If you think that you dare not, you don't,
If you'd like to win, but you think you can't,
It's almost certain you won't.
If you think you'll lose, you've lost,
For out in the world you'll find
Success begins with a fellow's will—
It's all in the state of mind.
Full many a race is lost ere even a step is run,
And many a coward falls ere even his work's begun,
Think big, and your deeds will grow; Think small, and you'll fall behind;
Think that you can, and you will— It's all in the state of mind.
If you think you are out-classed, you are;
You've got to think high to rise; You've got to be sure of yourself before
You ever can win a prize,
Life's battles don't always go
To the stronger or faster man;
But soon or late the man who wins
Is the man who thinks he can.

Wilson Family Tree

Charles Christian Wilson
B 17 July 1960
M 8 January 2017
Alison Mary Greig
B 15 July 1963

Brooks Christian Wilson
B 30 March 1933
M 18 April 1959
Christine Ann Meredith
B 22 August 1932
D 2 April 2020

John Christian Wilson
B 2 July 1962
M 25 February 2005
Susan Robinson

Emma
B 19 October 2006

Louisa
B 6 August 2010

Mary Meredith Wilson
B 15 March 1965
M 17 May 2003
Graeme John Familton
B 1 October 1954

Caleb John Familton
B 8 August 2004
Eli Joshua Brooks
B 7 February 2006
Eliza Mae Familton
B 17 February 2008

Andrew Christian Wilson
B 3 August 1967
M 22 November 1997
Frances Leigh Harrison
B 18 August 1968

Hugo Christian Wilson
B 28 January 2000
Anna Doria Wilson
B 27 June 2002
Lucy Valentine Wilson
B 11 November 2006
Charles "Charlie"
Christian Wilson
B 11 November 2006

Media Coverage

BHP'S GREAT LITTLE NON-CORE ACTIVITY

The benefits are only likely to increase from a BHP joint venture based on coal tar, which used to be a waste product. By PHILIP RENNIE

IN recent years, BHP has been unloading non-core businesses and investments. But it continues to hold a 50% shareholding in Koppers Australia, despite this being a minuscule asset by BHP standards.

Koppers Australia, which is little known outside trade circles, is an outstandingly successful coal-tar distillation business with strong growth prospects. BHP's investment in 1967 was $750,000, and no further capital has been required. BHP is receiving annual dividends of $1 million — a small payout from the Koppers profit of $11.4 million for 1994-95, of which half could be equity-accounted by BHP.

Profit will be up substantially in 1995-96 to nearly $14 million, or $20 million if the 20% shareholding in the United States company Koppers Industries Inc (KII) — which holds the other 50% in Koppers Australia — were equity-accounted. And strong growth is forecast to continue. Koppers executives in the US and Australia recently discussed strategies with the objective of 15% compound annual growth, and a target of $80 million profit for Koppers Australia by 2006.

There is another tie with BHP apart from the shareholding: Koppers Australia operates three ships, which are managed by BHP's shipping department.

If BHP ever wants to sell its shareholding, the Australian sharemarket undoubtedly would snap up a float. But a float of Koppers Australia seems unlikely. However, there might be another way in. KII is not listed but it is studying the possibility of making an initial public offering and listing on the US market. The presence of the British entrepreneurial investor Hanson Trust as a KII shareholder does nothing to diminish this prospect. If KII makes an initial public offering, US brokers might be surprised at the level of inquiry from Australia.

The name Koppers comes from the German chemist who invented the oven that heats coal to produce coke for steel blast furnaces. Coal tar, a residual product, is rich in chemicals. In the early 1960s, a BHP executive met a counterpart from the predecessor company of KII at Harvard University's advanced management course. "What do you do with your tar?" the Koppers man asked. The answer was that it was disposed of by burning in the blast furnaces. The outcome was the formation of Koppers Australia in 1967.

With feedstock from the ovens in which BHP makes coke for its blast furnaces, a coal-tar distillation plant was built near the Newcastle steelworks. Tar is brought from BHP's other steelworks in ships that heat the tar to keep it fluid. A tar distillation plant is similar to an oil refinery, taking feedstock and separating it into constituent parts. In recent years, demand for tar pitch in Australia has outstripped local supply, and Koppers Australia has been buying coal tar in China, Taiwan and Japan. Koppers Australia has

Brooks Wilson: "Aluminium gave us the cash to do other things"

bought coal tar from a big Chinese steel company since 1981, and shipped it to KII in the US.

Tar is distilled into tar pitch (used in aluminium smelting), creosote (a wood preservative that is also a source of the carbon black used in the manufacturing of rubber tyres), and naphthalene (a chemi-

cal feedstock). Tar pitch is the main product, accounting for about 40% of sales, followed by timber-preservation chemicals, treated timber (including Koppers Logs, which are used in landscaping), and carbon black.

The oil shocks of the 1970s constituted a turning point for Koppers Australia. Because oil-fired power stations became uneconomic, and aluminium smelting consumes vast amounts of electricity, much of Japan's aluminium smelting capacity was closed. Australia was in the box seat with cheap electricity from coal-fired power stations, and the growth phase of Australian aluminium smelting began. Further expansion in smelting capacity is planned. Every kilogram of aluminium metal requires half a kilogram of tar pitch, which is consumed in the electrical process. Koppers Australia has 90% of the Australian market.

The boom in aluminium led to development of the other businesses. The company that became the basis of the timber-preservation division of Koppers was acquired in 1973. There was more expansion in 1989, when the division joined with the British-based Hickson International, the world's biggest producer of wood preservatives, to form Koppers-Hickson Timber Protection. In 1984 a 51% shareholding in the carbon-black producer Continental Carbon Australia was acquired. The managing director of Koppers Australia, Brooks Wilson, says: "Every company needs something to launch it, and aluminium gave us the cash to do other things."

The aluminium boom provided the financial muscle to make another important move. In 1988, the predecessor of KII experienced a hostile takeover attempt. In response, a leveraged management buyout was mounted, with participation by Koppers Australia and a US investment company since acquired by Hanson Trust. Koppers Australia came out of the deal with 20% of KII's issued shares, but one-third of the voting shares. KII, based in Pittsburgh, produces coke for sale to steelworks and provides coal tar from its own ovens. It is the largest supplier of tar pitch for US aluminium smelters. KII also makes treated timber railway sleepers. Total sales are about $US500 million.

Wilson is seeking continued expansion in local markets for Koppers Australia but, to maintain high growth rates, opportunities will be sought to acquire coal tar in Asia and sell it in world markets. There is also potential for new processing facilities. There is an understanding with KII that Asia is Koppers Australia territory. In addition to China, expansion opportunities are being examined in Bangladesh, India, Indonesia, Taiwan and Thailand. ∎

Australian Government Award

HONOURS AND AWARDS

26 JANUARY 1981

APPOINTED A MEMBER IN THE GENERAL DIVISION OF THE

ORDER OF AUSTRALIA

BROOKS CHRISTIAN WILSON

C I T A T I O N

FOR COMMUNITY SERVICE.

Government House,
Canberra.   2600.

9 JAN 1981

Dear Mr Wilson,

Further to my earlier letter His Excellency the Governor-General has asked me to let you know that Her Majesty The Queen has approved your appointment as a Member in the General Division of the Order of Australia.

Your award will be published in the Press on Australia Day, 26 January 1981, and in the Commonwealth of Australia Gazette on the same day. It would be appreciated if you could continue to treat this matter as strictly confidential until the day of publication. From that date you will be entitled to use the post-nominal initials A.M. after your name.

In due course you will be invited to attend an Investiture at which you will be presented with your Insignia.

The Governor-General has asked me to convey to you his congratulations, to which I should like to add my own.

Yours sincerely,

(David I. Smith)
Official Secretary to the
Governor-General

Mr Brooks Christian Wilson,
49 Cherry Street,
WARRAWEE   N.S.W.   2074

APPENDIX 4

ACC Award

Australia-China Council

Stuart Simson
Chair

8 September 1999

PERSONAL

Mr Brooks Wilson AM
Former Managing Director
Koppers Australia Pty Limited
49 Cherry Street
WARRAWEE NSW 2074

Dear Mr Wilson

AUSTRALIA-CHINA COUNCIL AWARDS

I am writing concerning the Australia-China Council Awards, an initiative of the Council that recognises outstanding contributions and achievements by individuals from Australia and China in a number of areas of Australia-China relations. This is the inaugural set of awards and also commemorates the 50th anniversary of the founding of the People's Republic of China in October 1999.

The Council received a large number of nominations for the awards under the broad categories of culture, business, science & technology, and community/education from individuals who have been involved in Australia's relations with China since establishment of diplomatic relations. Eight recipients have been selected, with one from Australia and one from China representing each of the above categories.

Please address correspondence to:
Australia-China Council Secretariat
PO Box E73, KINGSTON ACT 2604 AUSTRALIA
The R G Casey Building, John McEwen Crescent, BARTON ACT 0221 AUSTRALIA
Telephone: 02 6261 3818, 02 6261 2351; *Facsimile:* 02 6261 2143
(From outside Australia): Telephone: +61 2 6261 3818, +61 2 6261 2351; *Facsimile:* +61 2 6261 2143
Email: auschina.council@dfat.gov.au